International Terrorism
current research and future directions

International Terrorism
current research and future directions

Alan D. Buckley
editor, Journal of International Affairs
Columbia University

Daniel D. Olson
editor, Journal of International Affairs
Columbia University

AVERY PUBLISHING GROUP INC.
Wayne, New Jersey

SPECIAL CONSULTING EDITOR
STEPHEN SLOAN, THE UNIVERSITY OF OKLAHOMA

BOOK COORDINATOR, ALICE AGOOS

Photograph for Article 6 reprinted by permission of the Consulate General of Israel in New York.

All other photographs reprinted by permission of United Press International.

Book Cover by Gerard Iervolino

Art Director Professor Karwoski

First published by the Journal of International Affairs, Volume 32/Number 1.

CONTENTS

EDITOR'S FOREWARD

On May 9, 1978, the bullet-riddled body of Aldo Moro was discovered in the back of an automobile by Italian police. The kidnapping and murder, which are typical of an increasingly violent political tradition in Italy and elsewhere, were attributed to the Red Brigades, a large, well-organized and armed group of ultra-leftist urban guerrillas whose membership, some authorities estimate, exceeds 1,500 individuals.

During the fifty-four days of the ex-Italian Premier's abduction, the Italian people, and indeed the entire world, were witnesses to an extraordinary series of events which in many ways illustrate the fundamental methods and objectives of modern terrorist groups: committing spectacular crimes, generating intense publicity, instilling fear in the public at large and reducing the credibility of government's power to control such acts. In the case of Mr. Moro, the Italian Government declined to negotiate with the Red Brigades under any circumstances, and responded instead with one of the most massive manhunts in history. Despite the consensus among most segments of Italian society that Mr. Moro's abduction was a despicable and monstrous act, some Italians criticized the Government's behavior as excessive and inept. Moreover, the pathetic letters written by Mr. Moro to many of his colleagues and associates in government, pleading for accommodation and his very life, underscored a great personal tragedy that was too often obscured by the shrill headlines in the world press. The combined forces of the Italian Government were insufficient to save Mr. Moro's life and, on May 10, the day after his body was discovered, literally thousands of newspapers and magazines across the world carried the gruesome photograph of Mr. Moro's crumpled body in the back of a stolen automobile, demonstrating the difficulty which modern and highly sophisticated states cope with acts of organized terror.

International Terrorism

Terrorism is the use or threat of violence to instill fear. When such violence has as its ultimate objective the intimidation, subversion or destruction of structures and processes of public authority, we speak of political terrorism. In nearly all cases of political terrorism, violence against individuals and property does not result in political change. Rather, the fear induced among influential segments of society may achieve what the terrorists themselves cannot: radical changes in the ways by which governments behave and, thereby, a loss of popular confidence and legitimacy in established patterns of order.

Political terrorism is by no means a new phenomenon. Walter Laqueur notes in his book, *The Terrorism Reader,*[1] that the *sicarii,* a highly organized terrorist group, was quite active in the first century A.D. Zealot struggles in Palestine. What is new with regard to political terrorism, however, is that today it is increasingly an international phenomenon.

Much of today's terrorism can be viewed as international in several respects. For instance, the *goals* of many terrorist groups are international, aimed at the creation of new states (the Croatian terrorists in Yugoslavia or the *Front de Liberation du Quebec* in Canada), the destruction of existing states (Fatah, the Popular Front for the Liberation of Palestine and the Popular Democratic Front for the Liberation of Palestine in the Middle East), the liberation of some territories from the control of other states (the Armed Forces for National Liberation of Puerto Rico in the United States and the Provisional Irish Republican Army in Northern Ireland), the subversion of particular regimes (anti-Castro exiles in Cuba) or the complete transformation of the world political order (the Red Brigades in Italy, the Baader-Meinhof Group in Germany and the Weathermen in the United States).

Because so many of their goals are international, the *audience* of terrorist acts is also global. The current state of communications technology, which permits instantaneous world-wide transmission of terrorist acts, is cited by law enforcement officials, scholars and even terrorists as the terrorists' most valuable weapon. If fear and intimidation are the terrorists' immediate goals, technology permits the achievement of these goals on a global scale. There are probably few people who did not see the last gruesome photograph of Mr. Moro and who were not impressed with the message of frustration and vulnerability that it conveyed.

Because their goals and audiences are international, the *targets* of many terrorist attacks are often international in nature. Hijacking international commercial airliners or kidnapping employees of multinational corporations are only two of the most obvious examples. Attacking diplomats in foreign missions, thereby embarrassing home and host governments alike, is another. The 1975 attack on the Vienna headquarters of the Organization of Petroleum Exporting Countries (OPEC) is a conspicuous example of how vulnerable international organizations may be to terrorism, and how much publicity can be gained for terrorist causes by disrupting their activities.

Today's terrorists are also globally *mobile*. Terrorists rely upon rapid means of transportation not only for the commission of their acts but also to escape punishment. The 1972 massacre at Tel Aviv's Lod International Airport, in which members of Japan's United Red Army managed to kill twenty-seven people and injure seventy-eight others, demonstrates the relative ease with which terrorists travel from one country to another. And in 1975, when Ilich Ramírez Sánchez (the infamous "Carlos") forced several high-ranking OPEC oil ministers to accompany him and his associates in an Austrian-provided airliner after the attack on OPEC headquarters, the jet gave the terrorists the means to quickly and successfully seek asylum in friendly countries, first Libya and finally Algeria.

But perhaps the most disturbing aspect of today's terrorism is the growing international *network* of individuals and groups engaged in such activities.[2] Although few of these groups share tactical objectives or ideologies, many of them do share resources, diplomatic influence, launching bases, training facilities and support from various governments. An international black market for sophisticated arms provides a central locus for people with similar beliefs to discuss common needs and objectives and, although there are no known international "master-minds" or central organization, the increasing professionalization of terrorists would tend to suggest closer international cooperation and collaboration among them in the future.

Examples of such international linkages abound. The Tuparmaros guerrillas in Uruguay set an example of terrorist organization and tactics for many other groups around the world. The United Red Army attack upon

Lod International Airport was coordinated with, and supported by, the Popular Front for the Liberation of Palestine. Some Italian officials believe that the Red Brigades may have been assisted by German terrorists in their abduction of Aldo Moro. And some American law enforcement officials have asserted publicly that the Weathermen may have received training from the Cuban *Dirección General de Inteligencia*. While there is no publicly available evidence to support the latter assertion, there is somewhat more evidence to suggest that the American government supported Cuban exile terror against the regime of Fidel Castro, and that the governments of Libya, Syria, Czechoslovakia, East Germany, North Korea and the Soviet Union may have provided training and arms to various European, Middle Eastern and Latin American terrorist organizations.

Terrorism and the Study of International Affairs

Terrorism is clearly an international reality in today's world. As such, it deserves, and has increasingly received, attention from scholars of international affairs. True, terrorism claims fewer victims than more conventional forms of warfare between states, and its ultimate impact upon strategic world politics and world order may be less than significant. Nonetheless, the modern state, with its increasing responsibilities for national economic and physical security, can ignore such acts only at the risk of losing credibility and popular support. But neither can any one state hope to control terrorist groups alone. International cooperation in regard to terrorism may be an objective necessity in today's world, a necessity unfortunately not easily realized as illustrated by the disagreements among the delegates of the United Nations *Ad Hoc* Committee on International Terrorism.

Scholarly approaches to terrorism have taken three basic forms, all of which are represented in this issue of the *Journal*: the historical, the normative/instrumental and the behavioral. The historical approach involves the collection of data on past acts of terrorism, often relating such acts to the unique socio-political characteristics of the participants and victims. The articles by Bard E. O'Neill and Richard N. Lebow present excellent historical narratives of Palestinian and Irish terror, respectively, while the article by Brian M. Jenkins uses past trends in terror to extrapolate future trends in such activities. The normative/instrumental approach begins with the attitude that terrorism poses a major threat to today's political order and proceeds to analyze and suggest means whereby such activities can be controlled or eliminated. The essays by Stephen Sloan, Paul A. Tharp, Jr., and Yonah Alexander deal, respectively, with the contributions that social scientists can make to law enforcement, possible legal regimes for the control of terrorist activities and the responsibility of the media in free societies to report terrorism, not encourage it. The behavioral approach is designed to isolate certain similarities and differences in terrorist organizations, capabilities, characteristics and tactics so that this phenomenon can be more objectively understood as a form of political expression and behavior, however repugnant it may be. The typology presented by Richard Shultz is an original and important attempt to classify and analyze terrorist behavior using rigorous scientific methodology. In addition to his historical narrative, O'Neill successfully applies this typology to the case of Palestinian terror in his essay. And, in his article on mass destruction, Robert K. Mullen dispassionately considers the range of weapons available to terrorists who seek to commit such acts and then evaluates the utility of these weapons in light of typical terrorist skills and objectives.

It should be noted that no analysis of international terrorism ever fits neatly into one category or another, and that various emphases are placed on these approaches in each of the essays presented there. This is probably as it should be, for all three approaches have much to recommend themselves; perhaps only through a combination of all can the phenomenon of international terrorism be better understood.

Hopefully, social scientists, governments and the public-at-large are attaining a more sophisticated and enlightened awareness of terrorism, the kinds of individuals who commit such acts and the causes of this behavior. Although terrorism must be condemned for the brutal suffering it inflicts upon innocent people, this suffering is insignificant compared to that resulting from conventional warfare between states, systematic government repression and even the distress occasionally caused by governments acting in good faith (consider, for example, the behavior of various governments and international organizations during the widespread famines and epidemics in Ethiopia during the early 1970s). Terrorists are not always base criminals, but are frequently well-educated professionals from prosperous backgrounds. And the cause of this activity is seldom violence for its own sake; rather, it may be a reaction to violent and systematic political repression or a particularly invidious form of extortion. While it is important that we not romanticize terrorism, it is equally important that this phenomenon be viewed in a way that reflects the complex nature of the world's political realities. We hope this issue of the *Journal* will contribute to such an understanding.

Alan D. Buckley

NOTES

1. Walter Laqueur, ed. *The Terrorism Reader: A Historical Anthology* (Philadelphia: Temple University Press, 1978), p. 7.

2. For an interesting discussion of this network, see Ovid Demaris, *Brothers in Blood: The International Terrorist Network* (New York: Charles Scribner's Sons, 1977).

Chapter 1

INTERNATIONAL TERRORISM:
Academic Quest, Operational Art and Policy Implications
Stephen Sloan

Introduction

No one likes to think the unthinkable—that some day they may face the terrorist gun, knife, or bomb. To a public both fascinated and repulsed by the carnage they often witness on the evening news, terrorism is something to be observed, not experienced. Skyjacking, kidnapping, and assassination attempts are often perceived to be a deadly game between authorities and terrorists, while the victims mutely await their uncertain fates.

The continuing incidents, however, have forced the public to begin to accept the reality of terrorism. There is grudging realization that the hostage taker or bomb maker can and will strike anywhere and that there are no safe havens for any individuals or groups.

Confronted with a growing recognition of the threat by the public, policymakers and law enforcement authorities are hard pressed to "do something" in the face of a new and often grimly imaginative threat to the public order. The politics of concern call for bold programs to meet a new challenge. Such concern may lessen after an effective military response, as illustrated by the operations of Entebbe or Mogadischu. At such times, the mass media often proclaims that "the war on terrorism" has been initiated and the public slips back into a false sense of security based on the impression that the proper response has been found and that terrorism is now under control. This sense of security often remains until another incident confronts a global audience who prefer "the resolution" of a conflict by "concrete" action to the uncertainty that some day they may become the victims of terrorism.

While the often uncoordinated "battle" between authorities and terrorists is waged, representatives of crucial groups are now only starting to define their respective roles and apply their particular skills to meet a threat that will most assuredly be with us and take on new forms in the immediate future. The rhetoric of concern is being replaced by a variety of activities on the part of members of the academic community, operationally oriented enforcement personnel, and policymakers who must do more than talk about terrorism. The progress these groups make both independently and in concert will be instrumental in helping to determine if effectively devised programs can be formulated and executed to better meet the present and future faces of international terrorism. The urgent need for crucial programs based on scholarly research, operational expertise, and incisive policymaking and execution is absolutely vital in view of the sobering degree of coordination and cooperation among terrorist groups who are now acting together in a global assault on the civil order.

The Academic Quest: An Old Tradition, a New Field of Inquiry

While the study of the role of violence in politics has its genesis in a very old tradition in the social sciences, and the examination of terrorism as an aspect of war or revolution has been recognized as a major area of comparative and historical concern, the study of international terrorism is of very recent vintage. It has only been in the last decade that discrete analyses concerning skyjacking, hostage taking, and nuclear and biological threats have taken place. This is to be expected for it has been in the last decade that contemporary terrorists have effectively employed a revolution in modern transportation and communication in the pursuit of their goals. Moreover, the terrorists now literally can strike virtually anywhere within a day and a half and almost immediately get their message of fear and intimidation across to a global audience. Terrorism may be an ancient phenomenon, but contemporary terrorism is indeed a new and frightful innovation in destructive capacity.

Faced with the emergence of a new form of terrorism, the academic community is now in the process of defining the characteristics of international terrorism in order to ascertain both the scope and method of their inquiry. This problem of definition is far more than an exercise in semantics. The formulation of definitions and the ascertaining of the characteristics of what has been variously called transnational or international terrorism is essential if guidelines are going to be established by which social scientists can collect and evaluate data on strife incidents. While there are certainly fundamental value questions related to ascertaining what is "terrorism," as contrasted for example to "criminality," a number of social scientists have preferred to leave the debate over issues of values to international forums. By establishing at least a minimum consensus on the elements of what constitute international terrorism, a number of concerned social scientists are now attempting to establish an effective framework to analyze this new form of civic strife. While the topic of terrorism is indeed inherently emotive, the fact remains that one can and must devise objective criteria to study incidents of terrorism in order to suggest alternative responses and policies.

Even here this quest for definitional agreement, if not precision, is now being extended in developing and refining classification systems and typologies that on one hand can limit the scope of the inquiry, but on the other provide a means by which more effective comparative analyses can be considered. The classic problem of finding commonality in the midst of outwardly diverse acts confronts those who are studying terrorism on a global perspective.

This search has been accelerated by the increasingly effective use of systematic methods to collect and consequently evaluate data on terrorist incidents in a coherent manner. While one cannot and should not expect that a specific overarching approach will ultimately be accepted by scholars concerned with a methodological orientation, it is a positive development to note that the various methodological techniques are increasingly being employed in order to ascertain common patterns of factors for evaluation. As a result, there is often a high degree of similarity in reference to revising the criteria for the selection of data and the conclusions of scholars who have worked independently on their respective projects. Because of the concern over scope and method, there is evolving a growing body of literature on international terrorism. While the emphasis on general descriptive studies and collected articles is readily apparent at this time, this is quite understandable because it clearly represents the trends in publication and study that characterize many new fields of inquiry. There are and will continue to be positive attempts to integrate the study of terrorism. In addition, the study of international terrorism is now in the process of being recognized and consequently legitimized within the disciplines of the social sciences and cognate fields as a specific area of inquiry much as was the comparative study of political violence a decade ago. It is hoped, however, that this recognition can promote an integration of knowledge without providing a proliferation of studies which may place more emphasis on the evolution of conventional wisdom as a substitute for a vital boldness of approach to meet a new threat.

From the Academic Quest to the Operational Art

The increased concern and refinement within the social sciences has been employed by personnel and organizations who must devise operational techniques to counter the threat or the actualization of incidents of terrorism. The need to promote a positive relationship between the academic and law enforcement communities is vital since both sectors share common problems and challenges. Just as a comparative scholar has been forced to redefine the scope of his inquiry and devise new methodological techniques, so must law enforcement personnel, concerned military officials, and members of the intelligence community redefine their own crafts to meet the tactical and strategic innovations that have categorized modern terrorist operations. Moreover, concerned operatives must not only be able to modify their techniques to meet the present threat but also prepare to evolve new responses to the changing configuration of international terrorism.

At this time, great emphasis has been placed on technological and practical responses to the threat or actualization of terrorist incidents. Stress has been placed on development of static defenses in the form of electronic surveillance equipment and related devices to harden the perimeters of potential targets. This emphasis on technology has also been carried over to the development of new means of communication and increasingly sophisticated weaponry to counter the rapidly expanding arsenal of the trained terrorist. The stress on innovative tactical responses has produced specialized police and military units which have had to redefine their roles and hence their training. The quality of these units varies markedly from various local forces which are given fundamental training in the rudimentary aspects of special weapons and tactics (SWAT) which are primarily directed at hostage situations, to the highly trained and professional units such as German Group 9 or the Israeli Commandos who have effectively brought the war home to the terrorist on a global basis.

In conjunction with tactical refinement, emphasis has been placed on developing and disseminating increasingly sophisticated techniques of hostage negotiation. The Dutch, British and selective American agencies have pioneered in developing this new approach and in disseminating a wide variety of training programs at all jurisdictional levels. While the techniques of hostage negotiation as they apply to hostage situations in general and terrorist incidents in particular are still a very recently devised skill, they are a step in the right direction. The procedure offers a vital option that can be employed in conjunction with the tactical military response.

In conjunction with the tactical and behavioral refinements employed by law enforcement agencies, there is a growing recognition that the entire spectrum of corporate security must be reoriented to meet potential threats on physical facilities and personnel. Consequently, more professional and effective training has been given to private security forces who must now move beyond basic plant protection from physical pilferage and white collar crime. They must develop both static defenses and effective initial responses to engage in holding actions until regular security forces can come to their aid in the event of a terrorist incident. In addition to protecting facilities, both corporate security offices and private firms are now beginning to provide basic security for personnel who are likely to be targets of terrorism. There are stepped-up efforts to raise the security consciousness of individuals who may be subject to kidnapping overseas when they are in the employ of multinational corporations. In addition, selected personnel are learning basic techniques of self-help, as illustrated by evasive driving courses, in order to respond effectively if they are involved in an incident.

The combination of tactical and behavioral refinement in both the public and private sectors must not only continue but must be updated to meet the everchanging configuration of terrorist tactics and targets. As the potentiality of incidents at nuclear and chemical installations becomes a disturbing possibility, both public and private forces must be prepared to meet the increasingly sophisticated technocratic orientation and targeting of the modern terrorist.

From the Operational Arts to the Questions of Policy Formulation and Execution

In the final analysis, the effective integration of the academic and operational dimensions of countering the threat of terrorism will only be effective if proper policy formulation and execution take place at the local, national, regional, and transnational levels. While there is clearly a growing recognition of a need for a coordinated approach to meet the threat of terrorism, the basic formulation and execution of policy at this time has essentially been on an ad hoc basis. The evolution of a cohesive response has failed to take place on a number of levels. On the level of international diplomacy, despite positive developments in reference to selective treaties dealing with terrorism, there is still virtually no agreement, much less a coherent international policy, to meet the threat of terrorism. While there have been positive developments in reference to specific individual incidents, as for example the denial of landing rights to terrorists and the successful military responses, the character of reaction is primarily based on the demands of the particular situation.

Regional concern and responses have become a valid counter to the threat of terrorism, particularly among the industrialized states that are often leading targets for transnational terrorism. This regional response will probably also be employed more extensively by selected Third World states that are now also becoming victims of terrorist threats.

In the final analysis, however, the character of national or international cooperation has been limited by diverse factors related to national interest at the very time when terrorist groups are cooperating in their own insidious forms of alliances.

Even if we could assume that the respective nation-states could agree on common approaches at any level, the fact remains that there will continue to be barriers to effective cooperation because of the arbitrary jurisdictional boundaries among respective authorities which have blocked the need for the effective exchange of information in reference to intelligence and tactics. While the contemporary terrorist is increasingly international, the response still tends to be inherently fragmented.

This lack of a coherent response, particularly in reference to the collection and evaluation of information, places a particularly heavy responsibility on those within the social sciences who study terrorism. They must provide a neutral framework where information can be shared, thereby providing an opening in the barriers to dissemination that often categorize the relationships among respective intelligence agencies who may not fully share information because of the high levels of security consciousness. While the emphasis on security, of course, is vital, there is a wide variety of open sources that are available for comparative evaluation that have not been subject to systematic distribution. To this end, such organizations as the British-based Institute for the Study of Conflict and the International Institute for Strategic Studies and the American-based Institute for the Studies in International Terrorism and the U.S. Institute for the Study of Conflict are providing a framework for the sharing of information among concerned scholars and policymakers. In addition, such organizations can assist all concerned parties in dealing with a wide variety of vexing issues related to terrorism, including the need to open up further discussion on such fundamental issues as the role of the mass media and the basic issue of reconciling civil liberties with protection of the community.

Conclusion

If the study of international terrorism does represent a new field of inquiry, it is because contemporary terrorists are indeed engaging in a new form of violence which calls for a level of cooperation among policymakers, academics, and the operatives who must meet the threat. The rhetoric of concern must increasingly be replaced by programs of concerted action. As the bloodletting continues, we can neither afford the luxury of leisurely academic discussion or the bureaucratic infighting that has often characterized not "the war on terrorism" but an often ineffective holding action.

Chapter 2

CONCEPTUALIZING POLITICAL TERRORISM: A Typology*
Richard Schultz

Introduction

Throughout history, the strategies and tactics of political terrorism have maintained a trenchant position in the political calculus within and between nations. However, since World War II, the practice of political terrorism has undergone a frightful proliferation at the national and transnational levels. Given this proliferation, and given the immense complexity of political terrorism, it would seem fruitless to attempt to analyze this process without first developing a systematic typology. Typology development is important, for it represents the first step in the process of theory building. According to Meehan, "scientific explanation requires the systematic ordering and classification of empirical data."[1] In the case of the study/analysis of political terrorism, such developments have generally not been undertaken. While an intense study has ensued this post-war proliferation of political terrorist incidents, the literature has been primarily descriptive, prescriptive and very emotive in form. Very few studies have approached the issue from a more analytical, theoretical, and objective position. In addition, one is hard pressed to locate studies aimed at developing typologies that lend themselves to the rigorous analysis of the various forms political terrorism has taken, to depict common linkages and specific differences. Given this deficit in the literature, the following exercise seeks to take the initial steps in constructing a more flexible and useful typology of political terrorism.

A Typology of Political Terrorism

Although the contemporary importance of the phenomenon of political terrorism and its impact at the national and transnational levels is undeniable, a review of the literature reveals a lack of concern with theoretical and conceptual issues. Before presenting the typology developed in this study, a brief review of the few classifications of political terrorism that have been conceptualized will be presented.

As a first step, it is necessary to define, in a generalized sense, what constitutes political terrorism. While definitions of political terrorism have been affected by journalistic license and value generated notions, certain scholars have presented definitions that are cast in a more rigorous and objective perspective. While the works of Thornton, Wilkenson, Crozier, and Walter meet these requirements of objectivity and rigor,[2] for our purposes, Brian Jenkins presents one of the more perceptive delineations of the characteristic attributes of political terrorism. According to Jenkins:

> the threat of violence, individual acts of violence, or a campaign of violence designed primarily to instill fear—to terrorize—may be called terrorism. Terrorism is violence for effect: not only, and sometimes not at all, for the effect on the actual victims of the terrorists. In fact, the victim may be totally unrelated to the terrorists' cause. Terrorism is violence aimed at the people watching. Fear is the intended effect, not the by-product, of terrorism.[3]

In essence, political terrorism is goal directed, employed in pursuit of political objectives. It is calcu-

---

*An expanded version of this paper was presented at the International Studies Association annual conference, Washington, D.C., February 22–26, 1978. It contains an examination of the role and effectiveness of terrorism in insurgency warfare. The insurgency wars examined include Greece, Malaya, the Philippines and Vietnam.

lated violence directed at affecting the views and behavior of specific groups. While we generally agree with this definition, there are certain points with which we would take issue. First of all, while the instilling of fear characterizes the use of terrorism by many groups, it is not the principal aim of all terrorist acts. Furthermore, such acts may have certain tactical and strategic aims quite remote from instilling fear.[4] Based on the above observations and a liberal borrowing from a recent government research study of international and transnational terrorism,[5] the following working definition of political terrorism is proposed:

> Political terrorism may be defined as the threat and or use of extranormal forms of political violence,[6] in varying degrees, with the objective of achieving certain political objectives/goals. Such goals constitute the long range and short-term objectives that the group or movement seeks to obtain. These will differ from group to group. Such action generally is intended to influence the behavior and attitudes of certain targeted groups much wider than its immediate victims. However, influencing behavior is not necessarily the only aim of terrorist acts. The ramifications of political terrorism may or may not extend beyond national boundaries.

While a workable definition of political terrorism may be drawn from the literature, no such useful developments exist in the area of classification. Furthermore, the typological schemes that have been conceptualized are very limited in scope, basically categorizing political terrorism into a two part typology—enforcement terror (employed by those in power), and agitational terror (employed by those aspiring to power).[7] Thorton utilized such a classification, as did Crozier and Walter. In his study, *Terror and Resistance,* Walter labels the two components of his typology, siege of terror (employed by rebels) and reign of terror (employed by those in power).[8] It should be apparent that a typology based on this ruler-ruled, rebel-regime dichotomy falls short of the classificatory specifications outlined above. It is too simplistic, fails to analytically differentiate within these two categories, and does not present related comparative variables that generate assayable hypotheses within and between categories. As a result of these weaknesses, Wilkenson sought "to construct a more flexible typology which is not rigidly tied to the ruler-ruled dichotomy and which encompasses terrorism which stems from motives other than revolution or repression."[9]

The Wilkenson typology divides terrorism into three generalized categories: Revolutionary Terrorism, Sub-Revolutionary Terrorism, and Repressive Terrorism. According to Wilkenson, Revolutionary Terrorism is directed at "bringing about political revolution," Sub-Revolutionary Terrorism "is employed for political motives other than revolution," while Repressive Terrorism is government directed terror aimed at "restraining certain groups, individuals, or forms of behavior deemed to be undesirable."[10] While this was an improvement over prior attempts at classification, the Wilkenson typology also contains a number of weaknesses. In the first place, there is no hint as to how an observer is to distinquish between Revolutionary and Sub-Revolutionary Terrorism. Second, while he does broaden his categories, he fails to precisely specify the boundaries of each, especially in terms of the internal-external environmental level. Finally, and most significantly, Wilkenson's three dimension typology is not accompanied by a set of variables that allows for more rigorous and discriminate classification. In addition, by developing a set of variables sensitive to the complexity of political terrorism within each category, as well adaptable to cross category comparison, one would be able to generate and test broader and more comparatively derived hypotheses.

With these rather elaborate but nonetheless important preliminary remarks over, we may now present our typology. In essence, we have attempted to take Wilkenson's three categories, partially re-conceptualize them, and then select a set of variables that may be operationalized in order to improve our understanding of political terrorism within and between Wilkenson's three categories. Definitionally, our three categories of political terrorism—Revolutionary, Sub-Revolutionary, Establishment—may be defined as follows:

Revolutionary Terrorism may be defined as the threat and/or employment of extranormal forms of political violence, in varying degrees, with the objective of successfully effecting a complete revolutionary change (change of fundamental political-social processes) within the political system.[11] Such means may be employed by revolutionary elements indigenous to the particular political system or by similar groups acting outside of the geographical boundaries of the system.

Sub-Revolutionary Terrorism may be defined as the threat and/or employment of extranormal forms of political violence, in varying degrees, with the objective of effecting various changes in the structural-functional aspects of the particular political system.[12] The goal is to bring about certain changes within the body politic, not to abolish it in favor of a complete system change. Perhaps the broadest of the three categories, groups included here span the political spectrum from left to right (i.e., ethnic, religious, linguistic, regional, anticolonial, secessionist, reactionary, restorationist, etc.). Such means are employed primarily by groups or movements indigenous to the particular political system, though similar elements beyond the system's geographical boundaries may also rely on such means.

Establishment Terrorism may be defined as the threat and/or employment of extranormal forms of political violence, in varying degrees, by an established political system, against both external and internal opposition. Specifically, such means may be employed by an established political system against other nation-states and groups external to the particular political system, as well as internally to repress various forms of domestic opposition/unrest and/or to move the populace to comply with programs/goals of the state.

Although a long list of possible variables could be selected, for the sake of parsimony, we have chosen seven: causes, environment, goals, strategy, means, organization, and participation. Together, they yield the typology of political terrorism presented in Figure 1.

As was noted above, the axiom that political terrorism is goal directed underlies the whole approach of this typology. Although various writers have attributed the use of political terrorism to various notions/forms of irrational behavior, it is our position that most extranormal political violence is employed to achieve certain political goals. Although certain forms of violence may result from irrational behavior, organized goal directed political terrorism does not fall into this category. We define goals and the other variables that make up this typology in the following manner:

Causes

Causes may be broadly conceptualized as any one or array of observable economic, political, social, and/or psychological factors. Conditions underlying the decision to resort to the use of extranormal political violence are quite varied and complex. These generalized causal factors may be subdivided into two categories: long-term factors (preconditions extending over a lengthy period of time), and short-term factors (igniting events). In the case of non-revolutionary terrorism, long-term causal factors might include prolonged societal inequities, political disfranchisement, or economic depression; while short-term causes could be the result of a rapid upsurge of ethnicity, relative deprivation, or government repression.

Figure 1. Typology of Political Terrorism

general categories / selected variables	CAUSES	ENVIRONMENT	GOALS	STRATEGY	MEANS	ORGANIZATION	PARTICIPATION
REVOLUTIONARY TERRORISM	Economic, Political, Social, Psychological factors	Internal (urban or rural revolutionary groups)	Long Range/ Strategic Objectives	Primary or Secondary role in the overall strategy	Various capabilities and techniques employed	Nature— degrees of organizational structures	Participant profiles
		External (autonomous non-state revolutionary actors)	Short Term/ Tactical Objectives				Leadership style/ attitude
SUB-REVOLUTIONARY TERRORISM	Economic, Political, Social, Psychological factors	Internal (urban-rural non-revolutionary) groups)	Long Range/ Strategic Objectives	Primary or Secondary role in the overall strategy	Various capabilities and techniques employed	Nature— degrees of organizational structures	Participant profiles
		External (non-revolutionary, autonomous, non-state actors)	Short Term/ Tactical Objectives				Leadership style/ attitude
ESTABLISHMENT TERRORISM	Economic, Political, Social, Psychological factors	Internal (repression of urban or rural opposition)	Long Range/ Strategic Objectives	Primary or Secondary role in the overall strategy	Various capabilities and techniques employed	Nature— degrees of organizational structures	Participant profiles
		External (aimed at other nation-states or non-state actors)	Short Term/ Tactical Objectives				Leadership style/ attitude

Environment

This concerns the various forms political terrorism can take within the typology's three general categories. Conceptualized on the basis of geographical spheres, these environmental variations may be broadly classified into internal environmental (within the nation-state) and external environmental (global, or systemic levels) categories. For example, in the case of revolutionary terrorism, internal variations include the use of varying degrees of extranormal violence by urban and/or rural movements, while the external variation would include such actions when carried out by basically autonomous, non-state, actors.

Goals

Goals are the objectives at which terrorism is directed, categorized in terms of long range (broader strategic objectives) and short term (specific tactical objectives) political ends. Political terrorism may be directed towards both types of objectives simultaneously. For example, in the case of revolutionary terrorism, the long range/strategic objective would be to assist in the overthrow of the established order, while short term/tactical objectives might include disruption of the government's controls, demonstrations of the movement's strength, and building solidarity within the movement. In this case, the goals are a reflection of the ideology underlying the movement.

Strategy

For our purposes, this may be conceptualized as the overall plan—all necessary actions, policies, instruments, and apparatus—for the achievement of one's goals. It entails the deployment of men, materials, ideas, symbols, and forces in pursuit of these goals. With regard to political terrorism, the issue to be determined concerns whether it constitutes the primary or secondary tactics in the overall strategy. For example, in rural insurgency strategy, political terrorism has tended to be relegated to a secondary tactical position, while in the urban guerrilla and transnational variation, political terrorism has been elevated to a primary tactical consideration, and, in certain situations, to the level of a strategy.

Means

Means are categorized as any and all capabilities and techniques utilized within the broader strategic framework to achieve the goals projected. Capabilities available may include the most primitive or the most sophisticated forms of weaponry, mobility, electronic media manipulation, tactical communications, etc. The techniques utilized can range from kidnapping, barricade and hostage, bombing, armed assault or ambush, hijacking, incendiary attack or arson, assassination, chemical, bacteriological or radiological pollution.

Organization

As a fundamental adjunct to political terrorism, organization provides the formalized structure utilized for the planning, coordination, and application of extranormal forms of political violence. The success or limitations in the use of such forms of violence will be determined, in part, by the nature of the organization. For example, in the case of rural insurgent movements, an essential feature in the use of political terrorism is its detailed preparation. The effective use of terrorism is predicated on a thorough knowledge of localities, people, customs and habits. In essence, a great deal of time is spent in preparation, and organization is inextricably linked to this preparation.

Participation

This variable is broadly conceptualized to refer to the type of individual who takes part in political terrorism, as well as the various types of political leaders who employ political terrorism to achieve their particular goals. Thus, with regard to the profile of the terrorist, pertinent factors to be examined include: age, social background, occupation, education, ideology, personality, and belief system. While many of these factors would also be pertinent to the examination of leadership involved, we would suggest focusing on the issues of "willingness to employ" and "attitude towards employing" terror and violence.

The initial steps in the construction of such a typology are encumbered with the paradoxical dilemma of selecting a group of variables relevant to each of the three categories of political terrorism and sensitive to cross category comparison, while maintaining a degree of parsimony. Though additional variables may be introduced as the result of future scrutiny and revision, we have sought, in this initial period, to conceptualize a classificatory scheme that is not too unwieldy. Intuitively, the variables selected are ostensibly relevant to each of the general categories, and in addition, lend themselves to cross category comparison. Whether this is the case will be determined only as the study/analysis of political terrorism continues. Only through the future application of this typology will explicit category differences and similarities, in terms of the seven variables, be revealed.

In addition to improving the typological literature concerned with political terrorism, we have sought to construct a typology that complies with Mayer's "criteria for useful classification" —exhaustive and precise, each category "defined in terms of the same criteria."[13] However, it must be recognized that the typology presented is only in its initial stages of development. As future improvements and revisions occur, it will become more consistent with Mayer's criteria. This matter withstanding, the typology does provide a framework from which the phenomena of political terrorism can be more systematically and analytically studied. In the first place, it does provide a general classificatory scheme into which most instances of political terrorism, as well as its underlying factors, can be placed. Within each of the three political terrorism categories, a number of interrelated issues can be examined, and additionally, as will be noted below, the typology lends itself to cross category comparison.

Second, the typology draws attention to the complex nature of political terrorism, and the various pertinent factors involved in such activity. Given the emotionalism, controversy, and outrage surrounding political terrorism, monistic explanations such as the notion that all those who resort to such tactics are "abnormal . . . in the sense of being psychologically disturbed,"[14] are pervasive in the literature. In fact, the literature in general has tended to be descriptive, prescriptive and obliquely emotive in form. Hopefully, this typology will move the study of political terrorism away from such subjective analysis.

Finally, a third attribute of this typology is that it's more than simply a device for pigeonholing data. Classifying data is only the first step in explaining and predicting social phenomena. In addition, from a well developed typology, assayable propositions can be derived. This will then result in the clarification of specific differences and similarities within and between the three terrorist categories. In effect, this suggests that once this skeletal typology is fleshed out, we will find that while the general categories tend to differ when compared as integrated systems of factors, similarities between categories will emerge in terms of specific variables. For example, with respect to manipulation of the media, little difference may exist between a conservative ethnic or regional sub-revolutionary group employing terrorism and a radical left terrorist group. However, in terms of long range goals and strategic objectives, significant differences will probably exist between two such divergent groups.

The type of propositions that can be derived from this classificatory scheme may be divided into six categories. First are propositions specifying relationships between the seven variables within each of the three categories. In other words, how are the seven variables interrelated within the different categories. Propositions at this level take a macro or holistic approach. Macro analysis "refers to taking social groups or systems as the basic unit of analysis,"[15] and propositions in

this category will be conceptualized at this level. For example, rural insurgency movements would be approached as a system in which the seven specified variables interact. The same approach could be taken toward sub-revolutionary groups and establishment regimes employing terrorism. A comparative-within-category corollary of this first set of propositions consists of the comparative analysis of different variations within each of the general terrorism categories. For example, within the general category of revolutionary terrorism, one might compare the urban variation with the rural variation. Likewise, within particularistic sub-revolutionary groups employing terrorism, comparison of linguistic, ethnic, regional, or rural variations might be undertaken. A comparative-between-category corollary of the first class of propositions consists of the comparative analysis of variations of political terrorism across the three general categories. Thus, one might compare various urban revolutionary terrorist movements, with various sub-revolutionary urban groups employing terrorism to achieve whatever ends they seek.

While these three types of propositions are derived at the macro level, the typology also lends itself to "middle range" or micro level analysis.[16] Given the problems of macro level analysis, aptly noted by LaPalombara,[17] a micro level approach may presently be more appropriate. Concurring with LaPalombara's position concerning the immediate need to pay "greater attention to 'partial systems,' or a 'segmented approach' to theory and research," we would suggest that until concepts are more clearly defined, the empirical data base broadened, and the gap between "theoretical concepts and what (can be measured) in the field" narrowed, political terrorism analysis should focus on the middle range of micro level.[18] The final three propositions lend themselves to the discovery of similarities and differences within and between categories at this level.

The fourth set of propositions focuses on a single or a few variables within one of the general categories of political terrorism. Examples are numerous and would include: the role of terrorism in the overall strategy of the PLO; the techniques and capabilities of the Japanese Red Army; leadership profiles of reactionary regimes relying on terrorist tactics such as the Chilean junta, etc. This is perhaps the most bountiful of all of the categories. A comparative-within-category corollary of this fourth set of propositions consists of the comparative analysis of a single or a few variables among variations within each of the three general categories. Examples would include the examination of the goals of various sub-revolutionary groups who employ terrorism; the role/type of organization developed by urban and rural revolutionary movements and the composition of their domestic base; or the nature of the tactics employed by regimes utilizing terrorism to maintain order. Finally, a comparative-between-category corollary of the fourth class of propositions would allow for the comparison of one (or a few) variable across the various categories of political terrorism. As with the other propositional categories, numerous examples could be cited, including a comparison of the tactics utilized by various revolutionary and sub-revolutionary groups who utilize terrorism.

In sum, it is apparent that once the typology has been fleshed out in terms of data classification, assayable propositions at both the macro and micro levels will emerge. While the matrix only suggests that the three general categories of political terrorism may differ, as well as share similarities, this will be determined only through future research focusing on the six classes of propositions discussed above. In addition to these propositions derived directly from the typology, a number of important tangential issues are also readily apparent. For example, there is the complex issue of how the international community is to respond effectively to the various forms of international terrorism, as well as possible future trends and new variations in international terrorism. Finally, it should be recognized that this is only the first cut in the development of a typology of political terrorism. Much work remains to be done before it meets the requirements of a soundly conceptualized typology.

Conclusion

The purpose of this study was to take the initial steps in developing a typology that will allow for the systematic and analytical examination of political terrorism, and from which assayable propositions can be derived. While much work remains to be done to flesh out, improve, and revise the typology, as well as develop the propositions suggested, hopefully, this study's focus on the analytical and systematic study of political terrorism is a step in the right direction. In particular, case studies must be examined before any final conclusions can be drawn.

NOTES

1. Eugene Meehan, *The Theory and Method of Political Analysis* (Homewood, Ill.: Dorsey Press, 1965), p. 40.

2. Brian Crozier, *The Rebels* (Boston: Beacon Press, 1960); Thomas Thorton, "Terror as a Weapon of Political Agitation," in *Internal War,* ed. by Harry Eckstein (London: The Free Press of Glencoe, 1964); E. V. Walter, *Terror and Resistance* (New York: Oxford University Press, 1969); and Paul Wilkinson, *Political Terrorism* (London: MacMillian, 1974).

3. Brian Jenkins, *International Terrorism: A New Mode of Conflict* (Los Angeles: Crescent Publications, 1975), p. 1.

4. I am grateful to Bard E. O'Neill of the National War College for these perceptive clarifying points.

5. _____, *International and Transitional Terrorism: Diagnosis and Prognosis* (Washington: Central Intelligence Agency, April, 1976), p. 8–10.

6. Extranormal forms of political violence would consist of very extreme and brutal tactics that would be considered even beyond the conventions of war if they were used in a declared war between two nations. Such acts are too numerous to list. Examples would include blowing up a school with children present, torture of political prisoners, kidnapping/execution, etc.

7. Thorton, p. 73.

8. Walter, Chapter 1.

9. Wilkenson, p. 35.

10. *Ibid.,* p. 36–40.

11. Definitions of political revolution are many and varied. We would subscribe to the eight dimension definition proposed by Mostafa Rejai. He summarizes the eight dimensions into the following brief definition—"Political revolution refers to the abrupt, illegal mass violence aimed at the overthrow of the political regime as a step toward overall social change." Rejai, *The Strategy of Political Revolution* (Garden City, N.J.: Doubleday and Co., Inc., 1973), p. 7–9.

12. These structural-functional or "body politic" changes will be left open ended at this point, for they include the vast multitude of demands articulated by all the various groups spanning the left-right spectrum, who may employ terrorism.

13. Lawrence C. Mayer, *Comparative Political Inquiry* (Homewood, Ill.: The Dorsey Press, 1972), p. 17–18.

14. Albert Parry, *Terrorism: From Robespierre to Arafat* (New York: The Vanguard Press, Inc., 1976).

15. Mayer, p. 162.

16. The term "middle-range" is borrowed from Joseph's LaPalombara's, "Macrotheories and Microapplications in Comparative Politics," *Comparative Politics* (October, 1968), p. 52–78.

17. *Ibid.,* p. 57–63.

18. *Ibid.*

Chapter 3

TOWARDS A TYPOLOGY OF POLITICAL TERRORISM:
The Palestinian Resistance Movement*
Bard E. O'Neill

Introduction

Political violence is hardly a new phenomenon in the Middle East. Indeed, for millennia men have engaged in armed struggle in order to satisfy their claims and ambitions. The *types* of wars they have waged have varied over the centuries, ranging from conflicts between major collectivities (empires, colonial systems, and nation states) to those involving small units such as tribal or insurgent groupings. Similarly, the *forms* of warfare have differed. Historical accounts are replete with references not only to conventional air, land, and sea battles, but also to guerrilla and terrorist activity.

The present, of course, is no exception. During the past 30 years, there have been several interstate conflicts involving regular armed forces, the most sanguinary being the Arab-Israeli wars, as well as a host of insurgencies in which terrorism and/or guerrilla warfare have been the principal means of combat. While much of the insurgent activity has been conspiratorial in nature (e.g., Ba'thist and Marxist revolutionaries in the Persian Gulf states, the Ikhwan or Moslem Brotherhood in Egypt, and various left- and right-wing groups in the Sudan), there have been four notable examples of sustained internal war in the past 10 years: the Kurdish insurrection in Iraq, the Dhofar uprising in Oman, the Spanish Saharan conflict, and the Palestinian resistance.[1]

Although in each of the four cases terrorism has been employed by the insurgents, closer inspection reveals quite clearly that the Kurdish *Pesh Merga*, the Popular Front for the Liberation of Oman, and the Polisario fighters in the Sahara have considered guerrilla attacks the most important and decisive means of struggle.[2] Equally important, their behavior, for the most part, has been congruent with their beliefs. With respect to the Palestinian resistance, however, there has been inconsistency among and within its organizations regarding the role and efficacy of terrorism. Yet, despite whatever doubts some Palestinian leaders may have evinced about the issue, the facts of the matter are that terrorism became a significant part of the Palestinian arsenal, especially between 1970 and 1973. Accordingly, this paper will concentrate on the Palestinian resistance.

The analysis of Palestinian terrorism undertaken herein is part of a larger comparative effort which seeks to create an intellectually rigorous typology of political terrorism. As such, it is but one of several case studies designed to flesh out a heuristic typology proposed by Professor Richard Shultz. If successful, the collective enterprise should provide scholars with a cross-cultural classification scheme that will facilitate subsequent steps in the process of scientific inquiry—i.e., hypothesis generation, hypothesis testing, and theory building and validation.

Shultz has suggested seven variables that may be used to distinguish categories of terrorism: causes, environment, goals, strategy, means, orga-

*This essay was originally presented at the annual meeting of the International Studies Association, Washington, D.C., February 24, 1978. The opinions and interpretations herein do not necessarily reflect the views of the United States Government nor the Department of Defense.

nization, and participation. Each of these will be addressed in turn. First, however, some historical comments about the background of Palestinian resistance are required in order to place the problem in better perspective for the reader.

The Evolution of Palestinian Resistance

The intersection of two nationalist movements, the Jewish and Palestinian Arab, has generated the problem which is the focus of this study. Essentially, the current dilemma centers around the fundamental fact that, since the creation of a British mandate in 1922, both Jewish and Palestinian nationalists have laid claim to the same geographic area that today is comprised of Israel, the Gaza Strip, the West Bank, and a small portion of the Golan Heights.[3]

Zionism and Palestine

The Jewish nationalist movement received its initial impetus from members of the diaspora in Europe at the end of the 19th century. In 1896, its founder, Theodore Herzl, published a book entitled *Der Judenstaat* which called for the formation of a Jewish state, hopefully in Palestine. After the idea was endorsed by the first World Zionist Congress in Basel a year later, the Zionists organized an extensive effort to persuade the major powers, especially Turkey, to adopt policies favorable to their aims.

Support from the Turks, who controlled the area, was crucial in view of the fact that permission for the immigration of a large number of Jews to Palestine was considered a *sine qua non* for success, given the Arab majority in the area. Though the Turks refused petitions by European Jews to purchase a large tract of land, limited immigration nonetheless commenced, thereby giving rise to protestations by local Arabs whose own sense of nationalism was beginning to crystalize.

When the British seized control of the area during the war, they, too, were subjected to Zionist pressures. On November 17, 1917, the British Foreign Secretary, Arthur J. Balfour, indicated in a written declaration that Britain viewed with favor the establishment of a national home for the Jews so long as it did not prejudice the civil and religious rights of the existing non-Jewish communities in Palestine. The vigorous efforts of the Zionists and continued immigration following the Balfour Declaration increased tensions in the area; and over the course of the next two decades the Zionists and Arabs clashed violently, not only

with the Mandatory Power but also with each other. Of the two nationalist movements, the Zionist was by far the more successful in that it proved able to create and sustain, although not without considerable effort and cost, a Jewish state (Israel). The Palestinian Arabs (hereafter referred to the Palestinians), by contrast, were denied concrete expression of their nationalism in the form of an independent state, because, unlike their Zionist adversary, they were plagued by inept political leadership, poor organization, strategic miscalculations, and a lack of resources.[4] Political and material deficiencies such as these played a major part in the genesis and outcome of the first Arab-Israeli war in 1948.

The Creation of Israel and the 1948 War

Throughout the history of the Mandate, commissions of various sorts had investigated the Palestinian problem, but the British Government, preoccupied with the Second World War, had postponed a major decision, confining itself instead to the lesser issue of regulating Jewish immigration. In the aftermath of the war, an enervated Britain, beset with economic difficulties, decided to turn what seemed to be an unsolvable problem over to the United Nations (UN). After several months of intensive and skillful lobbying by the Zionists, the UN approved a partition plan on November 29, 1947, which made provisions for both Jewish and Palestinian states.

When the Palestinians rejected the plan, fighting ensued between the two sides. Taking advantage of the absence of a UN plan to implement the partition, the Zionists seized the initiative by acquiring weapons and training the forces necessary not only to defend their communities, but also to sustain a state that would be established after the British withdrew in May 1948. On the other side, the Palestinians proved unable to mobilize and organize the capability necessary to undercut the partition plan. A poorly coordinated intervention by regular Arab military forces did not spare the Palestinians from a major defeat, the consequences of which they would suffer for the next 30 years.[5]

The Legacy of the 1948 War

Three specific outcomes of the 1948 fighting were especially significant for the Palestinians: the flight of the refugees; the expansion of Israel; and the extension of Egyptian and Jordanian control to the Gaza Strip and the West Bank, respectively.

The large exodus of refugees from Israeli-controlled zones was due to the convergence of several factors. Many Palestinians fled because of systematic and deliberate coercion by the Zionists while others merely followed the example of their own leaders who had departed. There were also cases of notables encouraging the people to flee in the belief that the exodus would only be a temporary situation. Finally, of course, there were the untold numbers who always seek refuge from the ravages of war. More important than the specific causes of the exodus, as far as this study is concerned, is the fact that hundreds of thousands were displaced and dispossessed.[6] For the next three decades most would languish in refugee camps in the Arab states contiguous to Israel, while the remainder would disperse throughout the Middle East and other parts of the world.

Though the members of the Palestinian diaspora were separated from their homeland, they did not forget it.[7] Yet, while the attachment to Palestine was kept alive, strengthened, and at times, idealized in the art, literature, and poetry of the Palestinians,[8] recovery was left to the Arab states. Thus, for the better part of twenty years, the Palestinians waited in vain for the Arab armies to transform their longing for return into a reality. Because the June 1967 war seemed to shatter that possibility permanently, a new generation of Palestinian leaders asserted itself. Determined to control their own destiny, they turned to the restive masses in the camps for support—especially the younger elements that had been socialized to hate Zionism and Israel.

The failure of the Arab states to regain the losses of 1948 was related partially to the second outcome of the 1948 war, namely, the expansion of Israel to a size far more viable and defensible than it was under the original partition plan. Taking advantage of breakdowns of cease-fire arrangements that punctuated the 1948 fighting, Israel seized the Negev and Upper Galilee, both of which were considered vital to its future security.

The death knell for the Palestinian state called for in the partition plan was sounded shortly after the final armistice by the extension of Egyptian administration to the Gaza Strip and the annexation of the West Bank by Jordan. This third consequence of the war meant the Palestinians were not only denied any form of statehood, but they also became the political pawns of the Arab states. Moreover, it made subsequent Israeli arguments that there is no such thing as Palestinian na-tionalism appear credible to some listeners.

Palestinian Nationalism: 1949–1967

Despite the desperate circumstances of the Palestinians after the 1948 war, the fires of Palestinian nationalism still flickered. Though a younger generation of leaders appeared in the 1950s, their dispersion had led them to identify with various ideological currents in the area (e.g., Nasserism, Ba'thism, Marxism). These conditions, as William B. Quandt has noted, "... did little to foster a sense of purpose and unity among the Palestinian elite."[9]

In the 1960s two major organizations emerged that sought to rectify this desultory situation—the Palestinian Liberation Organization (PLO) and Al-Fatah.[10] The PLO was established at an Arab summit conference in 1964 as the official voice of the Palestinian people, and shortly thereafter it proceeded to organize a military component, the Palestine Liberation Army (PLA). In spite of its claim to autonomy, the PLO was in fact, heavily influenced by Egypt. Since the PLO's main base of operations was the Gaza Strip, Cairo kept the organization on a short leash lest it cause problems with Israel at inopportune moments. Moreover, the PLA, equipped with tanks and artillery, had a conventional force structure which appeared anomalous for a contemporary liberation organization. Since both the linkage to Cairo and the conventional force structure resulted in a low level of insurgent activity, the PLO was criticized by a number of Palestinian organizations as being insufficiently revolutionary.[11] When war did come in 1967, Israel crushed the PLA with relative ease.[12]

Shortly after the formation of the PLO, the rival organization, Al-Fatah (hereafter referred to as Fatah), made its presence felt. Fatah was a strong proponent of irregular, rather than conventional, warfare as a means to liberate Palestine, regardless of the strategy and views of the Arab states. Hence, it spent several years following its formation in the late 1950s planning for guerrilla raids against Israel.[13] In 1965 Fatah carried out its first attacks under the name Al-Assifa (the Storm). According to Leila S. Kadi, this name was chosen so that in the event of a failure Fatah might continue its secret preparations for armed struggle.[14] Whatever the case, Fatah decided to continue using the appellation Al-Assifa, and the latter became synonymous with its military wing.

With the exception of Syria, the Arab governments surrounding Israel were either opposed or indifferent to *Fatah,* and many of its recruits ended up in Arab jails. Furthermore, there were a number of armed clashes with Jordanian and Lebanese forces which were seeking to prevent guerrilla raids from originating in their territories for fear of Israeli reprisals. This interference, plus the fact that *Fatah* was operating with a total strength of no more than 200–300 men, rendered it incapable of inflicting serious military damage on Israel. Despite such problems, *Fatah's* operations were nevertheless a factor which helped precipitate the June war.[15]

The June War and the Palestinian Resistance Movement

The war, of course, was a greater disaster for the Arab states whose armies emerged from the conflict in a state of defeat and disarray. While the outcome was a far cry from the war of liberation envisaged by the *fedayeen,*[16] it had the paradoxical effect of strengthening the latter. Two factors accounted for this: the general result of the fighting and Israeli occupation of several Arab territories.

The magnitude of defeat suffered by the Arab armies led Palestinian leaders to once again question the feasibility of conventional combat against Israeli forces. The thought of a regular armed confrontation with an enemy whose relative military strength had increased substantially as a result of the war seemed ludicrous. Minimally, such a course of action would require many years of preparation, years that the new, more militant *fedayeen* leaders believed they could ill afford to lose. Moreover, the Palestinians, along with many Arabs outside the resistance movement, felt a strong psychological need to redeem their wounded honor and dignity. In a military-psychological setting such as this, the renewed call for an active and immediate armed struggle using unconventional techniques became an increasingly attractive alternative strategy for many Arabs.

The receptivity to the notion of a people's war was further increased by the territorial and demographic changes affecting the area which Israel controlled. Prior to the war, the idea of conducting a people's war in Israel that relied on some 300,000 Arabs living amidst 2.5 million Jews seemed absurd. When the war ended, however, some one million Arabs found themselves under Israeli rule and the potential area of operations for internal warfare had expanded to include the oc-cupied territories as well as Israel. Consequently, many Arabs concluded that armed struggle, in the form of guerrilla warfare and terrorism, had become a more plausible course of action.

The Strategic Aim of the Palestinian Resistance Movement

Taking advantage of the new developments, the *fedayeen* moved with alacrity to commence guerrilla and terrorist attacks and to organize for a protracted struggle against Israel. As part of this effort, the Palestine National Council (PNC) adopted a Palestinian National Charter in July 1968 which, in a series of articles, formally codified the ultimate aim of the movement as the total liberation of Palestine from Zionist control.[17] It was beyond debate that the Palestinian aim was tantamount to the destruction of the existing political-social-economic system of the Jewish state. As a *Fatah* pamphlet put it:

> The liberation action is not only the removal of an armed imperialist base, but more important—it is the destruction of a society. [Our] armed violence will be expressed in many ways. In addition to the destruction of the military force of the Zionist occupying State, it will also be turned towards the destruction of the means of life of Zionist society in all their forms—industrial, agricultural and financial. The armed violence must seek to destroy the military, political, economic, financial and ideological institutions of the Zionist occupying State, so as to prevent all possibility of the growth of a new Zionist society. The aim of the Palestine liberation war is not only to inflict a military defeat, but also to destroy the Zionist character of the occupied land, whether it is human or social.[18]

Since the *fedayeen* considered the attitude of the international community to be important in the liberation struggle against Israel, they made a concentrated attempt to transform their pre-1967 public image as a group that merely wished to "throw the Jews into the sea" by stressing two points. First, non-Zionist Jews would be allowed to remain in the new Palestine and second, the new nation would be a "secular, democratic, non-sectarian state." Unfortunately for the *fedayeen,* there was sharp disagreement within their own ranks on both points, especially the meaning and implications of a "secular, democratic, non-sectarian state."[19] More specifically, there was (and still is) no agreement on the role of a Jewish population in such a state, the nature of that state's relationship to the Arab world, and the state's political-economic order (e.g., Marxism or some variant of Arab socialism).

Since the majority of Israelis considered Zionism the *raison d'etre* of their state, to speak of destroying it was to speak of eradicating Israel and its people. Thus, it was not surprising that the new *fedayeen* propaganda line had little impact within Israel and that the Jewish population remained distrustful, unresponsive, and unimpressed.

The Strategy of Protracted Armed Struggle

Since the Palestinians fully expected Israel and its international supporters to oppose strongly the political transformation called for in the National Charter, they reconfirmed their commitment to a strategy of people's war. Inspired by the Chinese Communist, Algerian, Cuban, and Vietnamese examples, the *fedayeen* argued that revolutionary warfare was a historically proven and tested means that would bring success against Israel. That is, by conducting a "protracted popular war of national liberation," by emphasizing "armed struggle," and by employing guerrilla, terrorist, and political-psychological tactics, the Palestinians contended they could succeed where the Arab armies previously had failed. While there was no agreement on precisely which of the revolutionary warfare experiences should be emulated or emphasized, there was an abiding faith that revolutionary warfare could and would succeed in the Palestinian situation.[20]

Of the specific *forms* of warfare associated with the strategy of protracted armed struggle, guerrilla warfare was singled out as being particularly important. Article 10 of the National Charter referred to commando action as the nucleus of the liberation war that had to be sustained and escalated by mobilizing, organizing, and unifying the Palestinians and the Arab masses.[21] Though the resources and forces of the Arab world were also considered important, the *fedayeen* recognized it would take a considerable effort to bring them to bear.[22] In the meantime, self-reliance was critical; after 1970, it became imperative.

Stages of the Conflict

A review of 10 years of *fedayeen* activity suggests three discernible phases in the conflict with Israel. The first, 1967 to 1970, was marked by an upsurge of both guerrilla warfare along the borders, especially the Jordanian, and terrorism within Israel and the occupied territories. Although there were some transnational terrorist incidents (hijacking and bombings), conducted, for the most part, by the Popular Front for the Liberation of Palestine (PFLP), operational emphasis during this time was placed on guerrilla warfare and internal terrorism.

As things turned out, a combination of factors—sound Israeli counterinsurgency practices, a poor physical environment, insurgent disunity, organizational deficiencies, and differences with the Arab States—undermined what success the *fedayeen* had enjoyed in 1968–1969. While the effectiveness of the insurgents had already begun to decline by the summer of 1970, the Jordanian civil war in September and the expulsion from Jordan in the months following the war dealt a crushing blow to the operational capability of the resistance.

Following the regroupment of its battered forces in southern Syria and Lebanon, the Palestinian leadership attempted to direct new attacks against Israel from across the borders. When such activity brought strong Israeli reprisals, Damascus and Beirut moved to curb guerrilla raids, with the result that the latter were reduced to sporadic forays. *Fedayeen* operational problems were further exacerbated by Israel's successes in uncovering and detaining both terrorist and political cells in the occupied territories. Thus, it was not altogether surprising that the Palestinian resistance entered a new phase in 1971–1973, that of transnational terrorism.

The outbreak of skyjackings, assassinations, letter bombings, and kidnappings abroad, which shocked the world over a 2-year period, was far more widespread than similar episodes in the previous period. In part, this was because the largest and most powerful organization within the PLO, *Fatah*, abandoned its previous aversion to transnational terrorism by sponsoring the notorious Black September Organization (BSO).[23]

Following its inception, the BSO, along with other groups, moved to extract revenge, release psychological frustrations, publicize the Palestinian cause, and compensate for political and military weakness along the borders and within Israel and the occupied areas by carrying out terrorist actions that victimized scores of civilians and innocent third parties. In response, Israel mounted a multi-faceted and systematic campaign involving diplomacy, military operations, enhanced security for its citizens abroad, and attacks against terrorists outside the Middle East.

In September 1972 the death of 17 Israeli athletes, taken hostage by BSO terrorists during the Munich Olympic games, led to major air strikes against *fedayeen* bases and naval installations in Lebanon and Syria.[24] Judging that retaliatory strikes would be insufficient, Israeli officials promised a continuous war against the terrorists, indicating that preventive measures would be taken wherever warranted in the world, including Europe.[25] An intelligence officer also informed an American news magazine that Israel was considering a counterterrorist campaign, using tactics as vicious as those of the Arabs.[26] Support for the latter came from one of Israel's most respected newspapers, *Ha'arez*, which urged the government to form a special network of terrorists which would not be restricted by the limitations of various authorities.[27]

In response to this and other domestic pressures, Prime Minister Golda Meir said Israel would track down terrorists wherever it could reach them.[28] To strengthen its defense against terrorists, three senior officials in the security service were dismissed for negligence and security of embassies was upgraded to the point where they became veritable fortresses.

On the diplomatic level, Israel actively sought to exploit the carnage of Munich by persuading European governments to curtail Palestinian activities, and threatening to abandon peace talks until the terrorist problem was dealt with.[29]

These steps failed to deter the *fedayeen,* and for the next thirteen months the Israelis and the terrorists became locked in a deadly cycle of violence. Letter bombs mailed to Jews were countered by letter bombs mailed to Arabs, and assassinations of Jews in Europe were answered by the murder of Palestinians, in what came to be known as the "war of the spooks." On the Israeli side, such efforts came under the direction of a special advisor to the Prime Minister (first Major General Aharon Yariv, and then his successor, Brigadier General Lior) and were reportedly carried out by Ha Mossad L'Tafkidim Meyuhadim (The Institute for Special Tasks).[30] Although Israel refused to acknowledge such activity, the arrest of two Israelis in Norway in July 1973, their admitted role in Israeli counterterror operations, and the expulsion of an Israeli security official for harboring them, merely confirmed what informed observers had known all along.[31] Aside from the violence, Israeli agents also penetrated Palestinian organizations and engaged in a war of nerves with their Palestinian counterparts by placing obituaries of men still alive in newspapers and sending

Arabs letters about their private lives.

While the war of the spooks was running its course, the Israeli military was also busy. In February 1973 Israeli commandos raided *Fatah* and PFLP bases in the Nahr al-Baddawi refugee camp in northern Lebanon, reportedly using maps and diagrams supplied by agents in Europe.[32] Two months later, in a raid which shook the PLO leadership, Israeli commandos struck in the heart of Beirut, killing three Palestinian leaders—Abu Yussef, Chairman of the PLO Political Department; Kamal Adwan, whom the Israelis claimed was responsible for terrorism within Israel; and Kamel Nasser, the official spokesman of the PLO. Although Arafat and the other leaders remained safe, Israel's capability to strike at the leadership was hardly lost on them.

Aside from the losses caused by Israeli countermeasures, there were factors at work within the Arab world which eventually produced second thoughts about the effectiveness of transnational terrorism on the part of the PLO leadership. For one thing, the negative impact on the Arab image that inevitably followed in the wake of sensational incidents greatly irritated moderate leaders such as President Anwar as-Sadat of Egypt, King Hussein of Jordan, and King Faisal of Saudi Arabia. Secondly, a number of BSO operations victimized the Arab states. The seizure and murder of American diplomats during March 1973 at the Saudi Embassy in the Sudan, for example, was considered an intolerable affront by both Riyadh and Khartoum. Consequently, the Saudis condemned the *fedayeen* and threatened to withhold badly needed financial aid, while the Sudanese castigated *Fatah* and publicly exposed the linkage between *Fatah* and the BSO.[33]

In reaction to the pressures emanating from the international community, important Arab states and Israel, the mainline of the PLO, led by *Fatah,* retreated from its support of transnational terrorism in the months preceding the October war, the exception being the seizure of Jewish hostages in Austria in September 1973.[34]

The Shultz Typology

Drawing on both the descriptive summary above and supplementary information, we shall analyze the use of terrorism by the Palestinian resistance in terms of Shultz's typology, beginning with his adaptation of Paul Wilkenson's three categories of terrorism. Shultz suggests that revolutionary terrorism involves the threat or employment of extranormal forms of political violence in order to effect fundamental change in the political system. Though there is some confusion over the precise meaning to be ascribed to the term revolutionary in the textual treatment, a clarifying footnote which cites Mostafa Rejai indicates that what Shultz has in mind is the use of illegal violence to change the political regime as a step toward ultimate social change. Implicit in this is the familiar distinction between political and social revolution. Within the context of the political system we are interested primarily with a change in the values and institutions (regime) which determines how policies and decisions are made rather than with specific individuals in power or particular policy outputs.[35]

Bearing this in mind, one may categorize the Palestinian resistance as a revolutionary movement, since its ultimate aim is to supplant Zionist values and institutions with values and institutions designed to assure Arab dominance. That is to say, exclusive Jewish control of Palestine will be replaced by Arab control. Moreover, though socialist thought informs the value systems of both parties, the Israeli variations tend to reflect moderate European thinking (especially democratic socialism), whereas the different types of Arab socialism that influence thinking within the Palestinian resistance (Marxism, Ba'thism, and Nasserism) are very much interwoven with Arab nationalist themes such as the quest for Arab unity and the related desire to build Arab power and strength. Thus, although both sides subscribe to socialism, the type of socialist order they envisage differs considerably because of the nationalist dimension.

As far as the related issue of democratic values and institutions is concerned, there is also a difference. Though imperfect (because of the second class status of the Arab minority), the present Zionist regime nonetheless reflects the Western commitment to individual freedom, the open interplay of parties, interest groups and the media, due process, and the like. On the Palestinian side, however, the meaning of democracy remains vague, and its normative and structural requisites receive little attention. While this makes it difficult to say what the new institutions of a Palestinian Arab state would be like and how they would function, one may speculate that the oligarchical arrangements which characterize present Arab political systems would probably be reflected in the establishment of some form of authoritarianism.[36] In sum, the type of regime which the Palestinians would impose would be so different from the existing Zionist one that such a change could only be described as revolutionary.

Since the Palestinian aim threatens the very existence of the Zionist regime in Israel, it is hardly surprising that the vast majority of Jews are staunchly opposed to its actualization. Under such circumstances, where persuasion is considered to hold out little or no hope as a means of change in the foreseeable future, the Palestinian resistance has resorted to "illegal violence" in the form of both terrorism and guerrilla warfare. Inasmuch as terrorism has been a particularly troublesome phenomenon, it deserves a more detailed and systematic examination in terms of causes, environment, goals, strategy, means, organization, and participation.

Causes

The resort to physical violence, including terrorism, by the Palestinians may be traced to both long- and short-term factors. With regard to the former, the relative deprivation of the Palestinians in exile (especially in the refugee camps) since 1948 looms most significant. No one who is familiar with the literature, art, and political tracts of the Palestinians or who has talked to those in refugee camps can fail to recognize the deep sense of loss that pervades the Palestinian community, a sense of loss that is as much psychological as it is economic and political. Economically, Palestinians contrast their often bleak and squalid situation in the refugee camps with previous assets (however meager or substantial) that enabled them to make a living; politically, they point to the denial of national expression in its modern form, the nation state, a situation that is all the more galling to many in view of the Jewish success along these lines; and, psychologically, they express a strong affection for "lost land" as well as a yearning to restore their honor and dignity. It makes little difference if outside observers attribute the Palestinian predicament, at least in part, to the blunders of the Palestinians themselves. In the Palestinian view, the culprits are the Western powers and Israel, a view that has become more prevalent in a younger generation whose socialization has been marked by an emphasis on material deprivations and ideological explanations.

The ideological dimension is associated with the gradual emergence of a new leadership elite in the 1960s. Unlike their traditionally oriented predecessors, the new leaders have not been fatalistic about their circumstances, nor inclined to rely on the Arab states to rescue them. Influenced by modern ideological thinkers, ranging from Franz Fanon, Michel Aflaq, Karl Marx, and V. I. Lenin, to Mao Tse-tung, the new elites contend that Western imperialism, of which Israel is merely an extension, is the fundamental cause of Palestinian suffering and deprivation. Moreover, though the exegeses of particular modern ideological thought systems differ, they all agree that it is within the capability of "oppressed" people to redress their situation by means of revolutionary violence. In other words, the new Palestinian elites subscribe to the notion that they can regain control over their own destiny. Thus, though specific strategies, tactics, and targets might differ, in part because of ideological differences, the intersection of relative deprivation and ideology has provided a volatile mixture underlying the Palestinian political violence over the past 20 years.[37]

In the 1960s, however, such violence was intermittent and subject to the controls of the Arab states (Egypt in the case of the PLO; Syria in the case of *Fatah*). The June war, however, changed all of this, leading to an upsurge of guerrilla and terrorist attacks conducted by independent organizations. By demonstrating the failure of the regular Arab armies, the outcome of the June war strengthened the argument of the new Palestinian leaders that reliance on the Arab nations was a non-starter. Consequently, the war functioned as an "accelerator" of Palestinian violence and thus may be viewed as a shorter-term cause of terrorism.

In actuality, the situation was even more complex because as *fedayeen* activity picked up, different organizations stressed different forms of violence. On the one hand, *Fatah*, the Syrian-sponsored *Sa'iqa*, and the Marxist Popular Democratic Front for the Liberation of Palestine (PDFLP) tended to stress political organization and guerrilla attacks rather than terrorism as the more effective means of carrying on the armed struggle, whereas, on the other hand, the PFLP and one of its offshoots, the PFLP-General Command (PFLP-GC), indicated their belief in the utility of terrorism. What's more, the PFLP carried its attacks outside the occupied areas and Israel to other Arab states and Europe.[38] While this was in part attributable to the PFLP's belief that revolution in the Arab world was a necessary precondition for the liberation of Palestine, it also seems that such actions were a function of its ongoing rivalry with *Fatah* to achieve ascendency in the movement. Within this setting, terrorism provided a field of activity that would keep the PFLP in the headlines and hopefully increase its recruits.

Although in the case of the PFLP, the longer-term factors of relative deprivation and ideology combined with the shorter-term factors of the June war and rivalry for hegemony within the Palestine movement to produce terrorism, it would be a mistake to overlook the actions of the Israelis in 1968–1969 as a contribution. Simply put, as the Israeli counterinsurgency efforts along the borders became more effective, it became more difficult and costly to carry out guerrilla raids. Under such circumstances, terrorism increasingly emerged as a less costly form of violence than guerrilla warfare.[39]

Israel's successful anti-guerrilla efforts also played a part in *Fatah*'s de facto terrorist operations. Though favoring guerrilla activity, *Fatah* nonetheless carried out terrorist actions within the occupied areas. Unlike the PFLP, however, it eschewed transnational terrorism. Two key reasons, it may be argued, accounted for this. First, was the fact that *Fatah* was able to establish its credibility by mounting guerrilla attacks in 1968–1969; second, *Fatah* had emerged as the *primus inter pares* in the Palestinian resistance movement. Since it received the lion's share of publicity inside and outside the Middle East, had the largest membership, was the most active, and controlled the largest block of votes in the Palestine National Council (PNC), *Fatah* did not require dramatic acts of transnational terrorism to sustain itself against rivals within the movement.

The Jordanian civil war of September 1970 altered this situation dramatically. Besides being a defeat for the resistance overall, it reduced the capability of *Fatah* considerably and created a crisis of confidence in the movement. The impact was especially severe because by the time of the war Israel had reduced *fedayeen* terrorism and political organization within the West Bank to negligible proportions and was beginning to make inroads in the Gaza Strip. As a consequence, *Fatah* found its ability to operate significantly circumscribed within the target area and along the borders. Not surprisingly, the leadership of *Fatah* and the PLO came under fire from left-wing critics who argued that the policy of temporizing with "reactionary" Arab states, such as Jordan, had produced the sad state of affairs. Threatened by defections and convulsed by internecine power struggles, *Fatah* turned to transnational terrorism by sponsoring the previously mentioned BSO. Hence, the erosion of *Fatah's* capability and influence and the resultant threat posed to its hegemony in the movement, which was caused by the civil war in Jordan, may be viewed as a short-term cause of its decision to engage in transnational terrorism.

By the summer of 1973, the benefits to *Fatah* of sanctioning transnational terrorism had come into serious question. Though dramatic incidents did keep the movement in the global press, the images and reactions generated internationally were increasingly negative as far as both the *fedayeen* and the Arabs in general were concerned. Since the Arab states not only saw their prestige suffer as a result of terrorism but also became direct victims in some cases, *Fatah* was subjected to pressures to terminate transnational terrorism, lest it lose economic and moral backing from key donors. Inasmuch as *Fatah's* residual, and still relatively dominant, influence within the movement was more dependent than in the past on benefactors such as Saudi Arabia, it could ill afford to ignore the warnings.

Aside from acts carried out by small maverick groups opposed to the PLO leadership and sponsored by militant states such as Libya, transnational terrorism had receded by the eve of the October war. Though there were a few external incidents after the war, most notably the Entebbe skyjacking in 1976, *fedayeen* terrorism increasingly took the form of attacks in Israel by units penetrating by land or sea from Syria and particularly Lebanon.

Although the terrorist operations inside Israel and the occupied areas between 1973 and 1977 were often similar in form, their purposes frequently differed, a situation that was largely the result of dissension within the PLO over whether or not to accept a Palestinian mini-state made up of the West Bank and Gaza Strip, which Egypt was supporting, or to reject any proposals short of the total liberation of Palestine as well as negotiations with Israel. The notion of a mini-state divided the resistance into two camps: the pragmatists who supported the idea (*Fatah*, the PDFLP, *Sa'iqa*) and the "rejectionists" who were adamantly opposed

(the PFLP, the PFLP-GC, the Iraqi-backed Arab Liberation Front, and the Popular Struggle Front). The issue came to a head in the early spring of 1974.

Both sides prepared working papers and engaged in heated arguments over the general question of PLO participation in peace talks at Geneva and the specific matter of the Palestinian state. In moves closely associated with the political infighting, the PFLP-GC and the PDF carried out bloody terrorist attacks in the Israeli border villages of *Qiryat Shemona* and *Ma'alot* during April and May.

At *Qiryat Shemona*, the PFLP-GC killed or wounded some 34 people, the explicit and acknowledged objective being the prevention of a peace settlement. One month later, terrorists of the PDFLP seized a school and, in an ensuing exchange of fire with Israeli forces, inflicted extensive casualties on hostage children. Unlike the *Qiryat Shemona* episode, the political purpose at *Ma'alot* appeared two-fold. First, the PDFLP wanted to increase the pressure for the inclusion of the PLO in peace negotiations at Geneva, and second, it wished to strengthen its own position and influence in the bargaining which was about to take place. At the same time, the PDFLP also hoped to free a number of *fedayeen* incarcerated in Israel.[40]

In essence, what had happened was that the perception that negotiations between Israel and the Arab states were entering a more substantive phase had triggered another struggle over power and influence within the resistance. The pragmatists, fearing that they might be ignored altogether in the diplomatic process, saw terrorism as the only way to demonstrate that they were a force to be reckoned with. Should the PLO lose out in the peace talks, the pragmatists would be discredited and no doubt replaced by the rejectionists. As far as the rejectionists were concerned, they viewed terrorism as a means to increase tension in the area and thereby undermine the peace talks. At a minimum, they felt that the PLO would be excluded from the conference table because of the anticipated emotional reaction by Israel to all Palestinian insurgents. The rejectionists also assumed—with good reason—that the seeds of their own demise would be sown in any settlement since there was no chance that a role for "radicals," committed to Israel's destruction, would be acceptable to Israel, the Great Powers, and the moderate Arab states. In short, the struggle and concern over control of the resistance was a short-term cause of internal terrorism in 1974 just as it had been a short-term cause of the transnational terrorism in 1971–1973.

To summarize, a combination of long- and short-term causes accounted for the terrorist activity of the PLO. Over the long term, relative deprivation and ideology were crucial factors; in the shorter term, the outcome of the June war, the constant struggle for power within the resistance, and the increasing effectiveness of the Israeli counter-insurgency program inside the occupied areas and along the borders were most significant.

Environment

Environment, according to Shultz, relates to the geographic locus of terrorism—i.e., whether it is internal or external. From the Palestinian perspective, internal means Israel, the West Bank and the Gaza Strip (Palestine) whereas external refers to operations outside of this configuration. Both areas, as noted earlier, experienced terrorist activity.

As it stands, the internal-external dichotomy per se tells us little about the nexus between terrorism and environment. This implies that either there is no relationship or that the term environment is perhaps defined too generally and loosely. A careful evaluation of both the literature on insurgency and the data in the Palestinian situation suggests that the latter is the case.

When dealing with the environment, analysts of insurgency normally concern themselves with the physical and human context of the conflict. Physical is usually taken to mean the conflict area's size, topography, and transportation-communications network; human refers to the composition of the population (e.g., societal cleavages, literacy, economic distribution, and so forth).[41] For our purposes, the question is whether or not any of these had a bearing on the occurrence of internal and external terrorism; the answer, in a word, is yes.

In the previous section the effectiveness of the Israeli counter-insurgency program was identified as a short-term cause of terrorism in that the Israeli success in neutralizing the political organization and guerrilla attacks of the fedayeen left the latter no violent alternative to terrorism if they wished to continue the "armed struggle." What was not pointed out at the time was that the physical environment greatly facilitated the Israeli task. In order to understand this, it is necessary to recognize that the physical attributes conducive to a protracted armed struggle emphasizing guerrilla attacks (a large area with rough mountainous and/or heavily foliated terrain and a poor road and communications network) simply do not obtain in Palestine, a point which Arab critics of the fedayeen have long recognized.[42] In fact, the small size of Palestine, its generally open terrain and the well-developed road network and communications facilities enabled Israel to employ its air and ground mobile forces with good effect against guerrilla units both within Israel and the occupied areas and across the borders. Since the physical features of the environment contributed to the effectiveness of the Israeli counterinsurgency effort, and since the counterinsurgency success was an important short-term cause of terrorism, the nature of the physical environment may be seen as a secondary short-term cause of terrorism.

As far as the human environment is concerned, the most salient feature is the centuries-old cleavage between Arabs and Jews, a cleavage that is based not only on cultural, linguistic and religious differences but also on an intermittent history of political and violent conflict. Where this comes into play is with regard to relative deprivation, a long-term cause of Palestinian terrorism. Simply put, the extant Arab-Jewish cleavage has provided the essential foundation upon which Palestinian perceptions of relative deprivation rest.

This brief evaluation of environment suggests two things. First, the environment is an important element underlying the occurrence of terrorism but only if it is reconceptualized along more familiar lines. Second, the importance of environment is closely related to the causes of terrorism. Accordingly, it could be treated as a secondary cause (physical with regard to the short-term factor of counterinsurgency effectiveness; human with regard to relative deprivation) rather than as a separate major variable.

Goals

Palestinian terrorism has served a number of aims. Over the long term, terrorism, along with political action and guerrilla warfare, has been viewed as a means to achieve the revolutionary goal of creating a secular, democratic, non-sectarian state in Palestine (or, if one prefers, destroying the Zionist regime). In the short term, however, specific acts of terrorism have had a variety of tactical objectives; and, in some cases, a single act has served several purposes simultaneously. A review of terrorism since the June war reveals the following primary short-term or tactical goals that, at one time or another, have motivated Palestinian actions:

a. publicizing the activity of the resistance or particular groups in the resistance in order to demonstrate that the movement as a whole or a particular organization cannot be ignored in a final settlement;

b. demonstrating the ability of the resistance to carry out successful actions in defiance of the enemy in order to gain both popular and external support;

c. demoralizing and discouraging supporters of the government from rendering assistance by creating a climate of uncertainty and disorder;

d. provoking Israel to adopt repressive measures against innocent, uncommitted Arabs in the hope that such measures will lead the latter to join or support the resistance;

e. publicizing the activity of a particular group in order to attract recruits which will strengthen the group's capability and influence vis-à-vis its rivals within the movement;

f. sustaining the existing membership in the resistance or a particular group by providing an outlet for the expression of violent activity by radicalized individuals who might otherwise leave the movement or group;

g. provoking Israel to retaliate severely against Arab states and thereby undermine diplomatic efforts to achieve peace;

h. dissuading moderate Arab regimes from making concessions to Israel; and,

i. weakening the government of one Arab state in order to contribute to its eventual demise which, in turn, will benefit a rival Arab state (the inter-Arab rivalry dimension of the Palestinian resistance). Particular terrorist actions may also be devised to accomplish secondary tactical aims such as the payment of ransom or the release of prisoners.

Ample illustration of the pursuit of the various tactical aims is not hard to find. For instance, the pursuit of objective a was quite clear in the PDF and *Fatah* raids inside Israel in 1974, while g was the PFLP-GC aim in the previously mentioned *Qiryat Shemona* incident. B, c, d, and e were concurrent aims of the terrorism inside Israel and the occupied territories during the 1967–1970 period. In the case of b, c, and d, there was explicit acknowledgment whereas in the case of e, the evidence was more inferential (i.e., the constant scramble by the groups to claim credit for the same act and to publicize their own achievements while denigrating or dismissing those of their rivals). With regard to objective f, the emergence, composition, and transnational campaign of the BSO speaks for itself. Objectives h and i, however, deserve more explication.

As far as h was concerned, skyjackings and bombings in Egypt, Jordan, and Syria, though not frequent, were designed to prevent concessions to the Zionist enemy. The bombings of the Semiramis and Intercontinental Hotels in Syria and Jordan respectively in 1976 by the dissident Nidalist (Black June) faction in Iraq were cases in point. However, the Syrian case also appeared to be an example of i. That is, the bombing was part of an ongoing series of terrorist attacks involving not only agents of the mutually hostile Ba'thist regimes in Damascus and Baghdad, which sought each other's demise, but also Palestinian groups backed by Syria and Iraq. The use of terrorism to accomplish objectives h and i was not surprising in view of the legacy of clashes between Palestinian groups supported by different Arab states that occurred periodically from 1967 to 1977.

With respect to the secondary tactical aims of terrorism, nothing needs to be said inasmuch as the public record is well known and filled with examples of demands for money or the exchange of prisoners for hostages.

What, then, are the theoretical implications of goals for the Schultz typology? The answer, it seems, is related to the common thread which runs through all the objectives, namely, the weak military capability of the resistance as a whole or of particular groups. That is, in all cases the underlying assumption appeared to be that terrorism could enhance the perpetrator's power and influence at the expense of one's adversary, be that adversary Israel, an Arab state, or another Palestinian group. Hence, the long-standing proposition of students of revolutionary insurgency that terrorism is "a weapon of the weak" is reaffirmed. Whether the same is true of "subrevolutionary" and "establishment" terrorism, and whether the pursuit of different tactical aims appear in the latter two cases and make any difference, must be left to the comparative synthesis which transcends and follows this particular paper.

Strategy

The general *fedayeen* commitment to a strategy of protracted armed struggle, which was discussed earlier, tended to obscure the fact that in reality there was a good deal of dissonance in the movement when it came down to specific models. For *Fatah,* the Cuban notion of gradually building a party organization after guerrilla activity and fighting had commenced (the military focus) was inspirational because it successfully overcame disadvantages similar to those facing the *fedayeen*—e.g., small area of conflict and small numbers of insurgents. One major difference, understressed or ignored by *Fatah,* however, was the fact that Castro started his revolutionary war against an adversary with weak political and military underpinnings. Since the Israeli regime, unlike Batista's, had firm foundations, an excellent military with high morale, and enjoyed popular backing from the Jewish population, the *fedayeen* could not hope to succeed with an abbreviated campaign of guerrilla operations and psychological pressures. Hence, if there was to be any hope of success, the Palestinians would have to plan for a revolutionary war of long duration and, in that situation, the Cuban model was not as relevant as the Maoist, Viet Minh, Viet Cong, and Algerian experience. To conduct an armed struggle along the lines of the latter models meant that substantial attention had to be paid to a number of complicated and interrelated factors (extensive organization, unity, and the acquisition of popular and external support). Moreover, great care was required to orchestrate the use of political and military resources in a sequence of stages—political organization and propaganda, guerrilla warfare, and mobile-conventional or civil war.[43]

Although many of the revolutionary leaders whom the *fedayeen* hoped to emulate had analyzed carefully the development of and problems associated with the various stages of protracted insurgency, the *fedayeen* did not appear to have given the matter profound consideration. But, this is not to suggest that no thought was devoted to the issue.

In 1968 *Fatah* indicated that the revolution was in a stage of hit-and-run tactics which was designed to avoid large losses while potential supporters were indoctrinated. In September 1969, it was suggested that this stage, the "strategic defen-sive," was about to be superseded by another phase due to the temporary occupation of the Jordanian village of *Al-Hamma* by some *fedayeen* units. During the same month a *fedayeen* spokesman went further and contended that the Palestinians had, in fact, entered into a new stage of "hit-and-run" tactics, a claim echoed in *Free Palestine,* which reported that the *fedayeen* were in a stage of "mobile warfare" that was characterized by capturing areas for several hours and then withdrawing. The PFLP, however, was not as sanguine about these claims and developments, a fact made explicit by its spokesman, Ghassan Kanafani, who referred to the state of the revolution as "stagnant."[44] To the outside observer, the PFLP assessment seemed the more realistic.

When *fedayeen* activity in 1968–1969 was analyzed in terms of the Maoist model, it appeared that the Palestinian commandos (with the exception of the PDFLP) had decided to engage in both terrorism and guerrilla warfare without the benefit of systematic political, psychological, and organizational preparation. This decision, which was more reflective of the Cuban military-foco, short-duration model than it was of the Maoist-Vietnamese type of protracted warfare, led to a host of problems. For one thing, the fragile *fedayeen* organization which had been created was neutralized with relative ease by the Israeli security forces. Closely related to the organizational failing was the inadequate political preparation of the people in the target area which precluded them from functioning as the water within which the fish (guerrillas and terrorists) could swim. Thus, although the *fedayeen* acknowledged the need for patience and commitment to a long struggle, they proceeded to act precipitously and unsystematically. By 1970 the claim of having entered a phase of mobile warfare had been proven hollow. If anything, Israel's destruction of the terrorist networks and its increasingly effective counterguerrilla operations, which forced the *fedayeen* into the interior of Jordan, suggested that Israel had seized the initiative.

Beyond the fact that the *fedayeen* had not assessed the progression of protracted warfare thoroughly and clearly, they did not agree on a basic organizational approach. For *Fatah* and some of the lesser groups, the military focus of the Cuban model was attractive because it was thought to avoid the unnecessary conflicts arising from the maneuverings of political parties and groups. For the PFLP and the PDFLP on the other hand, the idea of not having a tightly disciplined party in control of the revolution was considered a heretical and critical shortcoming. This basic disagreement, combined with other factors, precluded the emergence of a unified revolutionary movement and strategy. The result was that groups in the resistance proceeded to act upon different principles and assumptions and the movement as a whole took on an *ad hoc,* fragmented character, which, in the final analysis, proved to be its Achillles' heel.

The relationship between terrorism and strategy was somewhat confusing under such circumstances. As far as the Cuban and Maoist theories were concerned, terrorism was not especially important; political organization and/or guerrilla warfare were the principal weapons. Yet, although both *Fatah* and the PDFLP accepted the idea that terrorism was neither decisive nor particularly desirable, they both carried out terrorist attacks. The PFLP and the PFLP-GC, meanwhile, employed and justified terrorism from their inceptions. What was perhaps most striking was that the two insurgent strategies which the *fedayeen* touted were incongruent with the role that terrorism came to play in the resistance. Consequently, strategy had far less to do with *fedayeen* terrorism than the factors identified in previous sections. While it may have contributed to some of the internal terrorism designed to gain popular support and demoralize Israel from 1967–1971, the strategy of the *fedayeen* was too loosely conceived and inconsistent to provide a blueprint for the terrorism over 10 years. In fact, just as the political, organizational, and diplomatic aspects of Palestinian behavior seemed to reflect short-term tactical reactions rather than an enduring strategic sense of direction, so did terrorism.

Means

The Palestinians used a wide variety of means in their campaigns of violence. In both guerrilla raids in the border areas and terrorist incidents, the insurgents employed automatic weapons, grenades, explosives, bazookas, surface-to-air missiles (SAMs), and Katyusha rockets. In addition, a number of techniques appeared in the terrorist episodes over the years, including assassination, kidnapping, barricade and hostage taking, bombings, armed assaults, and arson.

What is perhaps most instructive about the means is the lower cost associated with terrorism

as opposed to guerrilla warfare. That is, the smaller scale of terrorist actions required less weaponry, a factor that was no doubt attractive to the *fedayeen,* who frequently complained about logistical deficiencies. It does not seem to have been mere coincidence that the transnational terrorism of 1971–1973 and the internal terrorism of 1974 came at times when the munitions stocks of the PLO had been depleted because of the conflict with Jordan and confiscations in Syria.

This situation, of course, helps to explain the point that terrorism is a weapon of the weak which was noted in the preceding section. Lacking the capability to sustain and increase guerrilla operations on a continuous basis, the *fedayeen* turned the assets they did have against soft, vulnerable targets such as civil airliners and ships, unguarded commercial offices abroad, and unarmed civilians.

Organization

The weakness of the Palestinians was not just a function of a lack of means; it was also the product of organizational shortcomings on the macro-level with regard to the structural attributes of cohesion and complexity. Unity, in particular, has been a most distressing problem for the Palestinians. Between 1967 and 1977 over thirty organizations emerged. Of these, the most important—*Fatah, Sa'iqa,* the PFLP, the PFLP-GC, the PDFLP, the Arab Liberation Front, and the Action Committee for the Liberation of Palestine—were divided by ideological, tactical, and personal differences as well as by their linkages with rival Arab states. Though many attempts were made to unify and integrate the groups within supraorganizational structures, such as the Palestine Armed Struggle Command, the Central Committee of the Palestinian Resistance, the Unified Command of the Palestinian Resistance, and the PLO-Executive Committee, disunity remained the normal pattern of relations rather than the exception.

If the *fedayeen* did not fare well with respect to cohesion, they did not do much better when it came to complexity. Although they did have the formalized apparatus of the PLO (the PNC, National Fund, Executive Committee, Central Council, News Agency, and so on) at central level and institutional control of the refugee camps in Lebanon and Jordan (until 1970), the *fedayeen* were unable to extend their structural presence to Israel and the occupied areas in any meaningful way. Thus, they were without the parallel hierarchies (or shadow governments) that play such a crucial role in protracted insurgencies. While it is true that the *fedayeen* were able to create small terrorist cells and networks, these were hardly an adequate substitute for parallel hierarchies; furthermore, they were often uncovered by the Israelis.

The organizational drawbacks of the *fedayeen* on the macro level were related to terrorism in two ways. First of all, the endemic disunity which plagued the resistance was a cause of the continuing power struggle which, as noted before, directly led to acts of terrorism. Secondly, the costs associated with disunity—in particular the sanguinary conflicts in Jordan and Lebanon, and the failure to organize effectively in the occupied areas—were major reasons for the weakness of both the resistance as a whole and specific groups; and, that weakness, as we saw earlier, was a factor contributing to terrorism.[45]

As for the micro-level, specific *fedayeen* groups did prove to be quite adept at planning and executing some very complex operations. In part, this reflected the fact that the smaller groups were conducive to the secrecy and coordination necessitated by terrorist actions. Otherwise put, terrorism was the only form of violence compatible with the organizational capability of the *fedayeen* after 1970.

Participation

The organizational failings of the *fedayeen* were largely responsible for another aspect of *fedayeen* weakness, namely, the inability to mobilize active popular support within the occupied territories. With its rudimentary structures being dismantled by the Israelis with ruthless efficiency by 1969, *Fatah* broadcast coded messages to its agents in the crucial West Bank area to withdraw to Jordan because their safety was in jeopardy.[46] By 1970 the Arab population was not only apathetic; it also contained a number of people who were spying for the Israelis. Two years later the Gaza Strip also lapsed into a period of relative quiescence.

Without the active support of the local inhabitants, the *fedayeen* were denied a critical element which both scholars and practitioners have considered vital for protracted insurgencies. The lack of popular support, then, provides another factor which explains the weakness of the *fedayeen* and their concomitant resort to terrorism.

Depite their failure to mobilize popular support

in Israel and the occupied areas, the *fedayeen* organizations were able to acquire enough members and support from the refugee camps in Lebanon, Syria, and Jordan to carry out sporadic guerrilla attacks, terrorist raids, and substantial political activity. Though most combatants and supporters came from the dismal environs of the refugee camps, this should not obscure the fact that many intellectuals were attracted to the movement. Since the Palestinian community was one of the better, if not the best, educated in the Arab world, the leaders of the movement were able to surround themselves with capable lieutenants and commanders.[47] The participation of educated Palestinians was important in two ways as far as terrorism was concerned.

In the first place, it was through the educational process that young Palestinians became more conscious of the putative causes of their misery and exile, namely Zionism, imperialism, and Arab "reaction." Along with the interminable accounting of Zionist sins, came the cultivation of a renascent Palestinian national consciousness and the idea that it could reach its fulfillment through violent action. When the portrayal of Zionism, imperialism, and Arab reaction as the quintessence of evil was juxtaposed with the belief in the effectiveness of action, it was not surprising to find that few *fedayeen* evinced much concern about the morality of either external or internal terrorism. Indeed, where there was debate, it tended to focus on its anticipated utility and costs, not whether it was right or wrong.

Summary and Conclusions

As the discussion above indicates, a number of variables accounted for Palestinian terrorism. In order to facilitate the comparison of this case with others, each of the variables was investigated in the sequence and along the lines suggested by Professor Shultz. At this point it is important to briefly recapitulate, integrate, and where necessary, reformulate the findings.

To understand Palestinian terrorism, one must return to its long- and short-term causes. With respect to the former, relative deprivation and ideology were identified as the critical operative factors; with respect to the latter, the June war, the struggle for influence and control within the Palestinian movement, and the gradually increasing success of the Israeli counterinsurgency program were singled out. The picture did not end here, however, because, as we proceeded to examine the other major variables, the data suggested a number of linkages with the causes. For instance, the evaluation of environment suggested that the Arab-Jewish cleavage was the underlying foundation for relative deprivation, while the poor physical setting for guerrilla warfare made Israeli countermeasures easier to effectuate. When we turned to goals, we found that in spite of their heterogeneity, the short-term objectives of the *fedayeen* organizations were all designed to overcome or offset capability deficiencies of the perpetrator relative to Israel or rival contenders for power and influence within the resistance. In continuing, we uncovered a number of reasons for the capability deficiencies, namely, an incoherent and poorly conceived strategy, organizational failures (disunity and the absence of a parallel hierarchy in Israel and the occupied areas), marginal active popular support (participation) in the occupied areas, and limited assets (means).

Though it is difficult to summarize precisely the complex interplay among the variables, the following reformulation of the antecedent sections may put the problem in better perspective. To explain the use and increased incidence of terrorism by the Palestinians after 1967, the central concern ought to be its causes. While relative deprivation and ideology remain as the long-term

aspects here, the short-term factors should probably be modified. Although the importance of the June war's outcome must be retained, because it increased the belief in the effectiveness and efficacy of insurgent warfare as the way to defeat Israel, the factors of successful Israeli counterinsurgency and internecine power struggles within the resistance might be replaced by the concept of capability reduction. Succinctly stated, revolutionary terrorism is associated with strong feelings of relative deprivation, an activist ideology which stresses violence as a necessary and effective means of removing the sources of relative deprivation, a historical event which increases the belief that insurgent warfare can be successful, and a reduction in the capability of the insurgent movement or one of its constituent parts which portends imminent failure and collapse of the entire enterprise.[48]

The value of Shultz's variables becomes obvious at this point, for they enable us to explain capability reduction. That is, when bad strategy, a poor environment, organizational defects, low active popular support in the target area, and limited means for conducting guerrilla warfare are combined with the effectiveness of the counterinsurgent side, we are able to arrive at a more comprehensive explanation of capability reductions and, in turn, terrorism.

NOTES

1. On the distinction between conspiracy and internal war, see Ted Robert Gurr, *Why Men Rebel* (Princeton, New Jersey: Princeton University Press, 1970), pp. 10–11.

2. There are almost as many definitions of terrorism as there are analysts of the subject. While many of these are very perceptive, they often fail to distinguish terrorism as a form of war from guerrilla warfare. My own view is that guerrilla warfare differs from terrorism by virtue of the fact that it requires larger operational units and, most importantly, is directed at uniformed combatants (the army or police) or material assets (power stations, roads, communications facilities, and the like). Terrorism, by contrast, involves cellular units, and is directed at noncombatants. Accordingly, insurgents may act as guerrillas or terrorists depending on their targets.

3. The precise boundaries of "Palestine" have varied throughout its history. Today, for instance, the Israelis would argue that from an historical point of view, the East Bank of the Jordan also should be considered part of Palestine.

4. The reader interested in the debate surrounding the nature and dimensions of Palestinian nationalism should consult and juxtapose the following: *Israel and the Palestinians: Reflections on the Clash of Two National Movements,* ed. Shlomo Avineri (New York: St. Martin's Press, 1971), and the lengthy review of the Avineri volume by Ahmad R. Haffar, in *Journal of Palestine Studies* (hereafter *JPS*), Autumn 1972, pp. 120–127.

5. A detailed study of Palestine, particularly the evolution of Zionism and its role in the area, is beyond the scope of this paper. The interested reader will find a burgeoning literature on various facets of the topic. The following are especially informative: *From Haven to Conquest, Readings in Zionism and the Palestine Problem Until 1948,* ed. Walid Khalidi (Beirut: The Institute for Palestine Studies, 1971), particularly the introductory section; J. C. Hurewitz, *The Struggle for Palestine* (New York: Norton, 1950); Christopher Sykes, *Crossroads to Israel* (New York: World Publishers, 1965).

6. The reader interested in the Palestinian viewpoint on this should consult Fayez A. Sayegh, *The Palestine Refugees* (Washington, D.C.: AMARA Press, 1952).

7. Rashid Hamid, "What is the PLO?" *JPS,* Summer 1975, pp. 90–91.

8. For one account of the psychological predicament of the Palestinians in exile see Fawaz Turki, "The Palestinian Estranged," *JPS,* Autumn 1975/Winter 1976, pp. 82–96. On their nationalist prose and poetry see John K. Cooley, *Green March, Black September* (London: Frank Cass, 1973), pp. 45–67.

9. William B. Quandt, et al., *The Politics of Palestinian Nationalism* (Berkeley, Calif.: The University of California Press, 1973), p. 50.

10. Fatah means "conquest" and is an acronym that reverses the order of the letters of the Arab name of the Palestine National Liberation Movement: *Harakat at-Tahrir al-Watani, al-Filistini.*

11. Hamid, "What is the PLO?" pp. 94–95.

12. Walter Laqueur, *The Road to War* (Baltimore: Penguin Books, 1968), pp. 67–74. The PLO's close ties with Egypt and its problems with other Arab states, especially Jordan, are revealed in the following polemical tracts by Ahmad al-Shuqayri: *Forty Years of Political Life on the Arab and International Scene* (Beirut: Dar al-Nahar, 1972); *On the Road to Defeat With the Arab Kings and Presidents* (Beirut: Dar al-Audah, 1972).

13. Michael Hudson, "The Palestinian Resistance Movement: Its Significance in the Middle East Crisis," *The Middle East Journal,* Summer 1969, p. 299, and Laqueur, *Road to War,* p. 68, place the origin of *Fatah* in 1956 while Abdullah Schleiffer, "The Emergence of Fatah," *The Arab World,* May 1969, p. 16, traces *Fatah* to a 1957 summer meeting of a dozen or so Palestinians on a beach near Kuwait City.

14. *Basic Political Documents of the Armed Palestinian Resistance Movment,* selected and translated by Leila S. Kadi (Beirut, Lebanon: Palestine Liberation Organization Research Center, December 1968), p. 18.

15. Fred J. Khouri, *The Arab-Israeli Dilemma,* 2d ed. (Syracuse University Press, 1976), pp. 234–241. Several smaller Palestinian groups also operated at the time, including Heroes of the Return (military wing of the Palestinian branch of the Arab Nationalist Movement), Youth of Revenge Organization (another ANM group), and the Palestine Liberation Front led by Ahmad Jibril.

16. A term, derived from the Arabic word *Feda* or sacrifice, means Men of Sacrifice. It is used to refer to all Palestinian insurgents, regardless of their organizational affiliation.

17. See the Palestinian National Charter, especially articles 1, 8, 14, 15, 19, 20, 21, 22, and 23, in *Basic Political Documents of the Armed Palestinian Resistance Movement,* pp. 137–142.

18. *The Liberation of the Occupied Lands and the Struggle Against Direct Imperialism,* pamphlet No. 8 in *Revolutionary Studies and Experiments,* pp. 16–17, n.p., n.d. Also quoted in Hudson, "Palestinian Resistance Movement," p. 299. *Fedayeen* statements and literature have been replete and consistent with references to the aim of destroying Zionism. See, for instance, *Free Palestine,* September 1970, p. 15; editorial in *Fatah* (Beirut), November 18, 1971; interview of Abu Ammar (Yasir Arafat) in *Free Palestine,* February 1971, p. 1: *Arab Report and Record,* No. 1 (January 1–15, 1969), p. 19 and No. 2 (January 16–31, 1971), p. 78; *The Daily Star* (Beirut), May 17, 1971.

19. Disagreement on the meaning of a "secular, democratic, nonsectarian state" has been clearly evident within *fedayeen* ranks, with some groups striving to give the concept a meaningful content and others choosing to use it merely as a slogan for assuaging world opinion. See, for example, the accounts of a symposium of six *fedayeen* organizations on the question of the democratic Palestine state entitled *The Democratic Palestinian State,* n.p., March 1970. The same account can be found in *Al-Anwar* (Beirut), March 8 and 15, 1970. See also *Free Palestine,* March 1969, pp. 6–8; *The New York Times,* September 16, 1969; *The New Middle East,* No. 19, April 1970, p. 6. For three articles critical of the concept of the democratic state as articulated by the *fedayeen,* see Y. Karmi (trans.), *Three Articles on the Arab Slogan of a Democratic State,* by Y. Harkabi, n.p., n.d. This booklet can be obtained from

the Embassy of Israel. The articles reproduced therein can also be found in *Ma'ariv* (Tel Aviv), April 3 and 17, 1970; July 10, 1970.

There has been inconsistency on the question of which Jews could remain in the new Palestinian state. While the most recent position of the *fedayeen* has been that any Jew renouncing Zionism could stay, there have been suggestions that only those who were there prior to 1917 or, alternatively, 1947, could do so. The 1917 date seemed to be implicit in article 6 of the Palestine National Charter since the section clearly states that only those who resided in Palestine prior to the "Zionist invasion" were acceptable. Since the "Zionist invasion" is generally understood to date to 1917, the conclusion is obvious. See *Basic Political Documents of the Armed Palestinian Resistance Movement,* p. 137. For references to the 1947 date, see the comments of a *fedayeen* leader cited in *The New York Times,* June 17, 1968; *Arab Report and Record,* No. 5, March 1–15, 1970, p. 164. On the indications that all Jews rejecting Zionism could stay, see ibid., *Free Palestine,* June 1970, p. 1; interview of Abu Omar cited in *Arab Report and Record,* No. 13, July 1–15, 1970, p. 402; Arafat's comments to C. L. Sulzberger in *The New York Times,* October 30, 1970; *Free Palestine,* April 1970, pp. 1 and 6; interview of Abu Omar in ibid., September 1970, p. 6. Perhaps the best source is the *fedayeen* statement entitled "Towards a Democratic Palestine," *Fatah* (Beirut), 1970, reprinted in *Arab Views,* February 1970, pp. 4–6. The sincerity of the willingness to accept all Jews renouncing Zionism appeared to be compromised, however, by the acknowledgment on page 6 that *Fatah* engaged in active negotiations with several Arab states to allow Jewish emigrants to return to their countries of origin.

20.   While some individuals and groups within the *fedayeen* movement seemed more inclined toward certain revolutionary models than others, there has been an attempt to study and borrow from all of them. That the Chinese, Cuban, Algerian, and Vietnamese experiences have influenced *fedayeen* thinking in a substantial way is evident from their publications, interviews, and statements. Of particular importance in this regard was a two-part series of pamphlets published by *Fatah* in Beirut and Amman, 1967–1970, entitled *Revolutionary Studies and Experiences.* The following pamphlets are part of the series: *The Chinese Experience, The Vietnamese Experience,* and *The Cuban Experience* in part one, and *The Vietnamese Revolution* in part two. More accessible commentaries on the influence of these models may be found in Y. Harkabi, *Fedayeen Action and Arab Strategy,* Adelphi Papers, No. 53 (London: The International Institute for Strategic Studies, December 1968), pp. 7–8 and 13–17; Tom Little, *The New Arab Extremists,* Conflict Studies No. 4 (London: Current Affairs Research Services Center, May 1970), pp. 11–12; the interview of George Habash cited in *Arab Report and Record,* No. 5, March 1–15, 1969, p. 112; the interviews of K. Kudsi (*Fatah*) in *Free Palestine,* August 1969, p. 6; and September 1969, p. 6.

21.   See *Basic Political Documents of the Armed Palestinian Resistance,* p. 138.

22.   Ibid. (article 15), p. 139; *Free Palestine,* June 1969, p. 1.

23.   After a period of political jousting in the wake of the June war, *Fatah* had joined and become the most important organization in the PLO.

24.   *JPS,* Winter 1972, pp. 158–160; *The New York Times* (hereafter referred to as *NYT*), September 9, 1972.

25.   *NYT,* September 22, 1972.

26.   *Newsweek,* September 25, 1972, p. 49.

27.   Cited in *Newsweek,* October 2, 1972, p. 30.

28.   Jerusalem Domestic Service in Hebrew, October 12, 1972, in *Foreign Broadcast and Information Service Daily Report, Middle East and North Africa* (hereafter referred to as *FBIS/ME*), October 13, 1972, p. H2. The issue of covert attacks against the terrorists outside the Middle East led to a debate over the prudence and effectiveness of such a course of action. See *JPS,* Winter 1973, pp. 142–149. In July 1973 Meir confirmed that Israel was fighting terrorists all over the world. See Jerusalem Domestic Service in Arabic, July 30, 1973, in *FBIS/ME,* July 30, 1973, p. H3.

29.   According to *NYT,* October 22, 1972, a number of Arab students were expelled from Europe and new security controls were directed at Arab travelers.

30.   See *NYT,* April 12, 1973; *Newsweek,* April 23, 1973, p. 35.

31.   See *The Times,* London dispatch in *NYT,* July 26, 1973; *NYT,* August 15, 1973.

32.   *Time,* March 5, 1973, p. 21.

33.   On the Saudi and Sudanese reactions to the Khartoum incident see *Al-Hayat* (Riyadh) as quoted in UPI Dispatch, *The Colorado Springs Sun,* March 5, 1973; Omdurman Domestic Service in Arabic, March 6, 1973, in *FBIS/ME,* March 7, 1973, p. T7; *NYT,* March 8 and 11, 1973.

34.   Although the interruption of Jewish immigration from the USSR was no doubt a tactical aim in this operation, its larger purpose remains conjectural. Inasmuch as it was engineered by *Sa'iqa,* the Syrian sponsored *fedayeen* organization which generally eschewed transnational terrorism, it is very possible that it was part of Syrian-Egyptian moves to divert Israeli attention prior to the October war. *The Sa'iqa* role was admitted by its leader, Zuhair Muhsin, during an interview which appeared in *Al-Anwar* (Beirut), October 11, 1973.

35.   See Richard Shultz, "Conceptualizing Political Terrorism—A Typology," pp. 7–8. On the distinctions among parts of the political system—regime, authorities, and policies—see Charles F. Andrain, *Political Life and Social Change* (Belmont, Calif.: Duxbury Press, 1971), pp. 137–144; David Easton, *A Systems Analysis of Political Life* (New York: John Wiley and Sons, 1965), pp. 171–219.

36.   Both the traditional-patrimonial and the mobilizational types of political systems in the Arab world are authoritarian in nature. Moreover, in reality features of the two tend to intermix. For example, although the rhetoric and structure of the Ba'th parties in Syria and Iraq suggest a commitment to revolutionary change, the loci of power remain in either an extended family (e.g., the Takriti clan in Iraq) or a religious group (e.g., the Alawi in Syria). With respect to the patrimonial systems such as Saudi Arabia, Kuwait, the Sheikdoms and Jordan, the primary aim of maintaining the rule of the royal families is considered to be partially dependent on the effective management of the modernization process that includes a more equitable distribu-

tion of wealth. Whatever the emphasis, traditional or modern, the common denominator is authoritarian rule.

37. The feelings of relative deprivation and attendant frustration of the Palestinians are readily observable to anyone who visits with them, especially those in the refugee camps. Since it is so well recognized, further commentary would merely belabor the obvious. Why it has led to aggressive violence is a more compelling question. The answer, in this analyst's view, has much to do with the ideological assumptions of the new generation of Palestinian leaders and their ability to convincingly communicate their case to the masses. The *Fatah* leaders believe that Fanon's notion of violence as the means of personal and national liberation from imperialism is directly relevant to their circumstances. The Marxist groups also accept the inevitability of violent struggle, although in their view it must take place within the larger context of a class struggle against "reactionary," nonprogressive Arab regimes which they see as supportive of Zionism. On the role of Fanon's thought in Palestinian thinking, see *Free Palestine,* March 1971, p. 6; Harkabi, *Fedayeen Action and Arab Strategy,* p. 14; Ehud Yaari, "Al-Fath's Political Thinking," *New Outlook,* November/December 1968, pp. 30–31. On the influence of Marxism-Leninism on left-wing *fedayeen* organizations, see *Basic Political Documents of the Armed Palestinian Resistance Movement,* pp. 143–247. For secondary sources see Gerard Chaliand, *The Palestinian Resistance* (Baltimore: Penguin Books, 1972), pp. 80–96; Robert Anton Mertz, "Why George Habash Turned Marxist," *Mid East,* August 1970, pp. 32–36.

38. On the differences over tactics, see Hudson, "Palestinian Arab Resistance," p. 299; *NYT,* March 2, 1969, section IV; Gaspard, "Who's Who Among Guerrillas," p. 14. Habash was not reticent about defending attacks on civilians and operations outside the Middle East. Indeed, he indicated they would continue. See *ARR,* No. 5, March 1–15, 1969, p. 112; *NYT,* March 4, 1969. PFLP statements corroborated Habash's public view. See *ARR,* No. 6, March 16–31, 1969, p. 133. Although *Fatah* officially disapproved of attacks on civilians, it carried out a number of raids against civilian areas, justifying them as reprisals for Israeli attacks on Arab civilians. See *Free Palestine,* June 1969, p. 23; Fatah General Command Operations Order 546, August 27, 1969, reprinted in *The New Middle East,* No. 13, October 1969, p. 4. For the PDF view see the pamphlet *On Terrorism, Role of the Party, Leninism Versus Zionism* (Buffalo, New York: Palestine Solidarity Committee, State University of New York at Buffalo, n.d.), pp. 2–5 (also found in the PDFLP paper *Al-Hurriya* (Beirut), September 12, 1969); interview with Secretary-General of the Central Committee of the Popular Democratic Front for the Liberation of Palestine, Nayef Hawatmeh in *An-Nahar* (Beirut), August 17, 1973 as excerpted in *JPS,* Autumn 1973, pp. 198–199.

39. Through a combination of techniques—security barriers, mobile operations, artillery barrages, air attacks, and commando raids across the borders, and, most especially, active patrolling and ambush operations—the Israelis not only inflicted heavy losses on Palestinian guerrillas but they also reduced the number

and effectiveness of *fedayeen* incidents by September 1970. Aside from the casualties inflicted by Israeli forces, the *fedayeen* also suffered at the hands of Jordanian and, sometimes, Lebanese and Syrian forces. The Arab states were motivated to restrict the guerrillas, at least in part, because of the collateral damage inflicted on their economies by Israeli retaliatory actions. On these points see Bard E. O'Neill, *Armed Struggle in Palestine* (Boulder, Colorado: Westview Press, forthcoming), chapters IV and VII.

40. At *Qiryat Shemona* the tactical aim of the PFLP-GC was the release of 100 insurgents held in Israeli prisons whereas the strategic aim, according to a PFLP-GC spokesman, was "blocking an Arab-Israeli peace settlement." See *NYT,* April 13, 1974. After the *Ma'alot* operation, by contrast, a PDFLP spokesman stated very clearly that disrupting the Middle East peace process was not the aim of the operation. See *The Washington Post,* May 16, 1974. In fact, there are reasons to believe that the PDF would have exchanged prisoners for the hostages. First of all, the PDFLP publicly supported a peace settlement; second, two months before, Nayef Hawatmeh, the PDF leader, had called for a dialogue with Israel in an interview published in the Israeli newspaper *Yedi'ot Aharonot,* despite anticipated criticism from the rejectionists; third, the PDF was generally opposed to terrorism; and fourth, there was a rather elaborate plan devised by the PDFLP to effectuate the exchange of hostages for prisoners. The carnage which in fact took place was due more to faulty communications between the terrorists and the Israelis and between Israeli commanders on the scene and cabinet officials than to anything else. See Summary of Findings of the Horev Committee, Jerusalem Domestic Service, *FBIS/ME,* July 10, 1974, pp. N3–N6; *The Jerusalem Post,* Weekly Overseas Edition, July 16, 1974.

41. On the environmental question see Mao Tse-tung, "On Protracted War," *Selected Military Writings of Mao Tse-tung* (Peking: Foreign Language Press, 1963), pp. 200–201; A. H. Shollom, "Nowhere Yet Everywhere," in *Modern Guerrilla Warfare,* ed. Franklin Mark Osanka (New York: The Free Press of Glencoe, 1962), p. 19; C. E. S. Dudley, "Subversive Warfare—Five Military Factors," *The Army Quarterly and Defense Journal* (U.K.: July 1968), p. 209; Otto Heilbrunn, *Partisan Warfare* (New York: Frederick A. Praeger, 1962), pp. 44–45; and Gurr, *Why Men Rebel,* op. cit., pp. 363–364.

42. See, for example, Naji Alush, *The Road to Palestine* (Beirut: Dar al-Tal'ia, 1964), as cited in Harkabi, *Fedayeen Action,* p. 18.

43. On insurgent strategies see Bard E. O'Neill, "Insurgent Strategies: An Examination of Four Approaches," in *American Defense Policy,* Fourth Edition, John E. Endicott and Roy W. Stafford, Jr., Editors. (Baltimore: The Johns Hopkins University Press, 1977).

44. *NYT,* November 1, 1968; interview of K. Kudsi in *Free Palestine,* September 1969, pp. 1 and 6; ibid., November 1969, p. 2; interview of Yasir Arafat in ibid., August 1970, pp. 1 and 6; *ARR,* No. 18, September 16–30, 1969, p. 402; No. 2, January 16–31, 1970, p. 81.

45. On organization and unity see O'Neill, *Armed Struggle in Palestine,* Chapter VI.

46. On *Fatah's* withdrawal order see *The Daily Tele-*

graph (London), November 26, 1969; *NYT,* November 26, 1969. Arab's spying for Israel prompted the *Voice of Assifa* to warn in July 22, 1968 that the traitors should surrender and stand trial or be killed. On the broadcast and other indicators of nonsupport, *see Arab Report and Record,* No. 14, July 16–31, 1968, p. 215.

47.   Mertz, p. 195, pointed out that most members of the left-wing groups were admittedly middle-class intellectuals. *LeMonde* (Paris), in a survey published on July 16, 1969, reported that of 1,000 *fedayeen,* only 6 percent were illiterate, whereas 54 percent had primary education, 32 percent secondary education, and 8 percent had been to a university. Even Moshe Dayan, in March 1969, called attention to the fact that many infiltrators were highly educated and more ideologically motivated than in the past. See *NYT,* March 9, 1969. A good summary and analysis of education in the Pales-

tinian exile community may be found in Ibrahim Abu Lughod, "Educating a Community in Exile: The Palestinian Experience," *JPS,* Spring 1973, pp. 94–111.

48.   There are, of course, two variations here. The first, and most easily understood, is capability reduction *vis-a-vis* the main adversary (e.g., the PLO's need to demonstrate its viability in the face of successful Israeli countermeasures). The second refers to terrorism rooted in internal struggles. Though power for its own sake may be important, it should be recognized that those individuals and groups struggling to control the overall movement do so because they believe that their strategic and ideological assumptions are critical to ultimate success. Hence, any threat to the continued existence of such individuals and groups is, *ipso facto,* a threat to the longer-term fortunes of the resistance as a whole.

Chapter 4

THE ORIGINS OF SECTARIAN ASSASSINATION: The Case of Belfast
Richard Ned Lebow

More than 1800 people have been murdered in Northern Ireland since 1969. Many of them were killed simply because they belonged to the "other side." This study will explore the reasons behind such killing. What are the political and social conditions associated with sectarian assassination? Who carries out such killing? What kinds of people are chosen for victims? Answers to these questions should provide insight into the dynamics of intense communal conflict.

Sectarian assassination may be defined as the premeditated killing of a member of the opposing community merely by reason of this identifying characteristic. Sectarian assassination is largely *impersonal*. The victim is killed not so much by reason of any personal attributes but rather as a representative of an ethnic, linguistic or religious group. The victim may be selected at random and be unknown to his killers. This kind of violence should be distinguished from most forms of political assassination where the victim is chosen because of his personal position, politics or influence over others.

Sectarian assassination can take many forms. It may involve the killing of an individual person or the slaughter of an entire community. The violence may be dramatic and short-lived or low level but chronic. Any typology of the phenomenon would have to consider the magnitude and frequency of violence, the number and nature of both the perpetrators and victims and the extent to which there was official sanction or even participation in the violence. Possibly there are interesting relationships between the origins of sectarian murder and its various manifestations. It is not, however, the purpose of this paper to construct such a scheme of classification. It is nevertheless necessary to note the variety and complexity of the phenomenon before proceeding to analyze only one case study.

Sectarian assassination in Belfast takes the form of low intensity warfare between the Protestant and Catholic communities. It has accounted for over thirty fatalities a month although the average monthly death toll is considerably lower. Most commonly assassination squads operate from automobiles and abduct or kill victims on the fringes of working-class ghettos. Abducted victims may be tortured before being executed. Para-military groups have also planted bombs in or near pubs frequented by the other side. Less frequently victims have been intercepted on foot by vigilante patrols.

Sectarian assassination has become increasingly endemic to Northern Ireland where it is both a cause and result of social disintegration. Yet, little has been written about the motives of the assassins or their mode of operation. Such research is understandably difficult to conduct and is not without its hazards. However, inquiries into the subject are by no means impossible as demonstrated by the excellent investigative reporting of the Belfast press corps. Press reports, police records, court proceedings and contacts within both communities enable the researcher to glean considerable knowledge about such murders. The author is currently engaged in such a study and this article, based on data gathered during the course of several field trips to Belfast which included contact with para-military groups, represents an initial exploration of the problem.[1]

Sectarian assassinations have occurred in all six counties of Northern Ireland but the vast majority have been carried out in Belfast, where Protestant and Catholic working class neighborhoods abut on each other. In other parts of the North such murders have also been concentrated in urban areas with mixed populations (e.g., Portadown, Londonderry). By way of contrast, killing of soldiers, and to a lesser extent policemen, has been more of a rural phenomenon. Almost half of the British soldiers killed in Northern Ireland met their deaths in South Armagh, a hilly countryside containing mostly farms and small towns. Given the concentration of sectarian violence in Belfast, as well as the practical difficulties involved in researching murders throughout the Province, this study has been limited to that city.

I: The Origins of Sectarian Assassination

Sectarian violence, including assassination, may be a tactic adopted by underprivileged communities to force a more favorable distribution of values within a political system.[2] The recent communal war in Lebanon, initiated by Lebanese Moslems and their Palestinian allies, is a case in point. Such violence may also be employed by those who have a vested interest in the status quo and feel threatened by change. Most anti-Black violence in the United States is motivated by such fears as is the use of terror by landowners in India to protect the caste hierarchy.[3]

Rosenbaum and Sederberg refer to this latter kind of communal violence, when carried out by unofficial persons, as social group control vigilantism. They and others observe that the catalyst for such violence is usually the attempt by a lesser privileged community to improve its position, generally at the expense of a more advantaged group.[4] The incidence of racial violence in the United States appears to bear out this contention. It has been most pronounced when Blacks appeared to be making visible improvements in their legal, social and economic status as was the case during Reconstruction, World War II and the 1960s.[5] Anti-Ibo violence in Nigeria in 1966 was similarly rooted in resentment of the tribe's successful economic penetration of the northern region of the country.[6]

The incidence of sectarian violence in Northern Ireland conforms to this pattern as well. For almost fifty years, from the partition to the imposition by Britain of direct rule in 1972, the political structure of Northern Ireland had preserved Protestant political and economic domination in the small corner of Ireland where Protestants are in the majority.[7] The minority was also controlled through the application of what Catholics call "law and Orange Order," so named because the Royal Ulster Constabulary (RUC) has traditionally drawn most of its recruits from among members of the Orange Lodges. The RUC and the part-time militia, the B Specials, were the military arm of the dominant Unionist party. Both forces were well armed (the Specials were finally disbanded by the British government in 1969–1970) and over the years showed little compunction about using their weapons. They also intimidated Catholic voters during elections and individual Specials upon occasion engaged in the Northern equivalent of "nigger bopping." On Saturday nights, after a few drinks too many, they would go out and beat up a Catholic. This violence was especially pronounced during the years 1938–1940 and 1956–1962, periods in which Protestant anxieties were aggravated by IRA bombing campaigns.

The civil rights movement of the late 1960s triggered off even more violent reprisals. Civil rights marchers were assaulted by Protestant vigilantes with increasing frequency. Catholic neighborhoods were attacked by mobs, houses burned out and their residents encouraged to flee the country. This violence, obviously designed to intimidate the Catholic community, reached its peak in the "Battle of Bogside" in August 1969, a three day siege of the Catholic quarter of Londonderry which forced the British government to send troops into Northern Ireland.

The imposition of direct rule from London in March 1972 brought about a significant shift in the focus of violence emanating from the Protestant community.[8] Henceforth, political violence was increasingly directed against governmental authority in the form of coercive general strikes, the creation of barricaded "no go" areas and occasional confrontations with the British army. The objective of such violence was, as before, to protect the status quo, in particular to demonstrate to the British Government that further concessions to the Catholics would not be tolerated.

1972 also marked the advent of a new form of violence directed against the Catholic community: sectarian assassination.[9] Unlike the anti-Catholic violence which proceeded it, sectarian assassination in the context of contemporary Northern Ireland cannot be described as a form of social group control vigilantism. To the contrary, it is quite apparent to para-military groups on both sides that it is counter-productive of this goal.

Beating up or killing members of a defenseless community may serve as an effective form of intimidation. Killing representatives of a well-organized and militarily powerful community merely functions as a provocation. If anything, such violence is likely to promote greater communal solidarity facilitating even more militant action. This was indeed the case in Belfast. By 1972 the Catholic quarters of the city were organized and armed. IRA units manned barricades along the perimeters of these districts and their authority within was effectively unchallenged by either the army or the police.[10] The practical effects of a concerted effort by Protestant extremists to assassinate Catholics was only to strengthen the IRA by dramatizing the need for protection to Belfast's Catholics. These killings actually became an important prop for the Provisional IRA, a fact acknowledged by the Protestant extremists themselves.

Given the general recognition of the fact that these assassinations have actually played into the hands of the IRA, the student of Irish affairs must look toward explanations other than intimidation to explain this phenomenon. This most important is probably the *sense of rage and frustration* felt within the Protestant community.

The dramatic transformation of the political structure of Northern Ireland threatened by the civil rights movement aggravated the long standing Protestant paranoia about the Catholic community. This paranoia was deliberately encouraged by extremist politicians anxious to ride to power on the strength of a communal backlash. There was accordingly little attempt on the part of most Protestants to understand Catholic protest as a response to the pervasive pattern of discrimination against Catholics in every sphere of Northern life. Instead, the creation of "Free Derry" and Catholic "no go" areas in Belfast in 1969 and the commencement of the Provisional IRA bombing campaign in 1971 were interpreted by Protestants as part of a concerned Republican campaign, financed and supported by the South, to destroy Protestant political and religious liberties.[11]

Even more horrifying in Protestant eyes was the apparent success of the Republican effort. The very first civil rights marches had led to British in-

tervention in the form of pressure on the Northern Irish government to promulgate reforms designed to placate Catholic opinion. Catholic demands (e.g., reform of the franchise, allocation of public housing on the basis of need, dissolution of the B Specials) were seen to strike at the very foundation of the political system and were accordingly resisted by successive governments. The pressure from London mounted despite the increasingly violent nature of the protest and led to the imposition of direct rule in March 1972. By then, Northern Ireland resembled a war ravaged community, its streets and lanes patrolled by soldiers and the hearts of its cities blasted into rubble by bombs.

The inability of the security forces to stop the bombings and, worse still, their apparent unwillingness to enter areas openly controlled by the IRA, infuriated Ulster Protestants, many of whom began to speak of a sell-out of Britain. Such talk became even more common after prime minister Heath dismissed the provincial government and assembly and assumed responsibility for Northern Ireland's governance. The Protestant community felt helpless and vulnerable to the whims of a British parliament and government perceived to be unfamiliar with and unsympathetic to their plight. Not surprisingly, conversations with Protestants in the aftermath of direct rule revealed a widespread sense of anger and frustration. Some of this fury found release in attacks on Catholics, which began in earnest in the Spring of 1972.

The expression of Protestant rage in the form of sectarian killings must also be understood in terms of the military dilemma faced by Protestant activists. IRA violence has been directed principally against the RUC, British army and central business districts of Northern cities, all of these realistic pressure points for an organization striving to force a British withdrawal from Ireland. Protestants, by way of contrast, have no such obvious targets save IRA cadres which they found difficult to identify and attack. They were thus reduced to striking out against the Catholic community as a whole and whose opposition to the status quo and support for the IRA was taken for granted by Protestant militants. Sectarian assassination became a surrogate for more effective kinds of political-military action.

Sectarian assassination has also served as a means of advancing the political objectives of para-military organizations. Para-military bodies in Northern Ireland depend upon high levels of communal tension and fear for their very existence. The violence has therefore been self-serving in a very direct way.

The IRA, for example, was militarily moribund until the summer of 1969 when its membership increased several fold in response to Protestant mob assaults on the Bogside in Londonderry and Catholic districts in West Belfast. Arms searches and army-IRA clashes further exacerbated tensions and strengthened the IRA, especially the break away Provisional wing which began its reprisal campaign against the British army in March 1970. The killing of British soldiers provoked a rapid escalation of the conflict and led to the introduction of internment by the British which more than any other policy generated support for the Provisionals. The IRA has accordingly thrived in an atmosphere of Catholic insecurity, a situation its leaders have deliberately sought to create. The same is true for Protestant para-military organizations.

The Ulster Defence Association, the largest Protestant para-military body in Ireland, was organized to provide protection to Protestants from the IRA. Its growth was given a great impetus by the imposition of direct rule in March 1972 which, as noted earlier, triggered off Protestant fears of a sell-out by London. The UDA is currently the *de facto* authority in many Protestant neighborhoods of Belfast. Its leaders are vying with middle class politicians for control of the Protestant working class, the very core of Protestant power in the province.

The influence of Protestant para-military organizations depends upon the level of insecurity within the Protestant community *and* the inability of the middle class politicians to work out a viable political solution to Ulster's problems. Communal violence, and sectarian assassination in particular, helps to insure both objectives. Sectarian killings provoke counter measures from the Catholic community which in turn exacerbate Protestant insecurity and reliance upon para-military bodies for protection. Sectarian killings also have the effect of polarizing both communities thus making any political solution more difficult to achieve.

Evidence in support of the contention that sectarian assassinations are in part motivated by such political objectives can be adduced by examining the incidence of such killings. During the last three years assassinations of Catholics have been especially pronounced prior to and during negotiations between representatives of

the two communities. Most recently, there has been a spate of such killings associated with the Northern Ireland constitutional convention, the latest attempt by the British government to encourage a negotiated settlement of Ulster's political future.

Some of the better documented cases of organized sectarian murder also point to the conclusion that such violence is meant to influence public opinion. The murder of three Southern musicians by the UDA in the summer of 1975 is a case in point. The plan, which backfired, was to intercept the van carrying the group back to the Republic after a Northern engagement and blow it up with the musicians inside, making it appear as if they were smuggling explosives across the border. The bomb exploded prematurely killing two of the UDA men along with three of the four musicians. Confronted with the evidence, the UDA admitted that the object of the attack was to dramatize Southern complicity with the IRA and thus force Protestant delegates to the constitutional convention to take a harder line.[12]

Breakaway factions of the Provisional IRA have also carried out sectarian killings to prompt a harder line within the Republican community. Breaking truce between the Provisionals and the army has usually been the objective of such violence. A recent incident for which such a group claimed responsibility occurred in Bessbrook, County Armagh, a town with a history of excellent communal relations. On January 5, 1976, a bus bringing home both Catholic and Protestant working men was stopped by a renegade IRA group and the ten Protestant riders were mowed down by machine gun fire.[13] The killers hoped to provoke Protestant retaliation forcing the Provisionals in turn to break their truce. Extremists on both sides have a common interest in stoking the fires of communal discord by carrying out sectarian killings.

Revenge has also become an increasingly important motive for sectarian assassination as such murders have increased. The Provisional IRA never sanctioned sectarian killing; they executed people for specific offenses, usually suspicion of informing. However, the number of sectarian assassinations carried out by Protestants in the Spring of 1972 led to a growing feeling within the IRA that something should be done to deter and avenge such killings.

The first revenge murders were carried out by the Provisionals on July 1. Two Protestants, aged

30 and 34, had spent that evening in a UDA "Shebeen" (illegal drinking club) in Alliance Avenue. They were picked up by Catholic vigilantes while walking home along Oldpark Road near the Catholic Bone area and were handed over to the local Provisional brigade. Their bodies were found the following afternoon in the nearby Cliftonville Cricket Ground. Both corpses showed signs of physical abuse, probably the result of interrogation, and had numerous bullet holes in the neck and head. Later that month the Provisionals killed more Protestants for purposes of revenge.[14]

The IRA killings only intensified the activities of Protestant assassins, now equally intent on achieving revenge. This tit-for-tat response led to a spate of sectarian killings on both sides, there being seventeen alone in the month of July. Henceforth, the incidence of sectarian killings increased dramatically as the murders assumed a logic of their own. The effect has been to so terrorize the two communities that unorganized mobs have sometimes meted out revenge without any immediate provocation. One of the more vicious instances of this occurred in August 1975 when a Protestant maintenance worker drove his truck into a Catholic district of Belfast to deliver hardboard for repairs to houses damaged by bomb blasts. After making his third delivery he was surrounded by a mob, dragged from his truck and, screaming with fear, was beaten and shot to death.[15]

Sectarian assassination also functions as a means of establishing control over the rank and file of loose knit para-military bodies. Murder and torture violate social norms in Belfast as well as the law. This gives para-military bodies leverage over those members who participate in such activities. Such activity can also create certain kinds of bonds among the participants which may be exploited by leaders to advance personal or organizational goals. Dostoevsky's *The Possessed* provides an insightful exploration of such techniques of social control. The story of Charles Manson offers an equally chilling modern example of this process.[16]

Violence appears to be consciously exploited as a technique of internal cohesion by Protestant para-military organizations. The IRA seems to have much less of a need to rely upon such a means of control. The reasons for this probably stem from the very different organizational framework of the IRA, whether Provisional or Official. The IRA and its components resemble a military organization. Until recently there has been a formal structure, hierarchical control—albeit not always effective—and a notable *esprit de corps*. IRA violence reflected these attributes: it has generally been authorized from above, has had specific political objectives, and has been carried out in a comparatively professional manner.

By way of contrast, Protestant para-military bodies more closely resemble gangs. Indeed, many of their activities (e.g., extortion, protection rackets, petty larceny) are more criminal than political. The structure of such groups is loose and informal despite the use of impressive sounding military titles. Authority is exercised largely on the basis of personal charisma and internal discipline and cohesion appear to be a major problem. Here, sectarian murder often plays a role.

It is not unusual for Protestant assassination squads to include a young recruit who is given the task of actually carrying out the killing. The act of murder ties him to the group. It is also a ritual means of proving his method, not dissimiliar in function from the Plains Indian taking his first coup or the young Masai warrior killing his first lion. Torture may perform a similar function. Many Protestant groups maintain "romper rooms" where abducted persons are interrogated or errant members punished. One member of a para-military body described to the author his participation in a session where each member had to stab the victim in order to demonstrate his commitment. The victim, repeatedly brought back to consciousness by doses of cold water was in such agony that he pleaded with his torturers to kill him.

These interrogation sessions frequently involve considerable mutilation of the victim. One of the earliest known instances of such torture involved a 48 year old Catholic killed by a UDA unit in the Shankill in August 1972. His body, found in a doorway along Oldpark Road, had over 150 knife wounds covering every part of his anatomy. The wounds were actually small nicks designed to cause pain and were apparently administered while the victim was suspended from a slowly tightening noose with which he was ultimately strangled.[17] Subsequent victims have showed signs of sustained beatings, electric shock and branding with hot irons.

A further cause of sectarian assassinations must be sought in the realm of psychopathology. The general breakdown of social order in parts of Belfast has encouraged deeply disturbed persons to act out hitherto repressed fantasies. This often occurs within the framework of para-military organizations where such acts are given political rationalizations. One such case involved the killing in July 1972 of a 15 year old mentally retarded Catholic in his home, off Oldpark Road, by four UDA men. In the early hours of the morning the four broke into the house, located in a Protestant street, pistol whipped a Protestant lodger, gang raped the widow who owned the house in front of her son, and then shot them both. Fortunately, the woman survived and her testimony helped to convict the culprits.

It is interesting to note that the Loyalist reaction to the crime was that of revulsion, Belfast being one of those places in the world where rape is seen as a more heinous crime than murder. The four convicted men were beaten up in prison by other Loyalist prisoners and the ringleader had to be held in solitary confinement for his own protection.[18]

Despite such revulsion, the growing incidence of particularly brutal torture and senseless killings suggests that para-military bodies, especially on the Loyalist side, have made little effort to weed out seriously disturbed persons from their ranks. In fact, their presence, sometimes in positions of authority, may contribute significantly to the level of sectarian violence.

II: The Killers

Successive British ministers have referred to sectarian assassins as depraved human beings. For evidence, they point to the cases, some of which were described above, of particularly barbaric killings. This characterization is comforting in that it is difficult and even more chilling to imagine sane family men going out to murder people almost at random. The validity of the description is, however, an altogether different matter.

Evidence about the personality structures of sectarian assassins is naturally difficult to come by. For the most part, it must be based on the psychiatric examination of culprits brought to justice, hardly the best sample. The few psychiatric reports which are available do not suggest any pattern of mental disturbance, a finding, for what it is worth, that supports the author's view that the majority of sectarian assassins are not mentally disturbed.

Judging from those convicted, Protestant assassins tend to be young single males who are unskilled or unemployed. Their average age is twenty-two. Most had poor school records and some previous history of trouble with the authorities. The picture that emerges is that of young men who are marginal to the society. They realistically perceive few opportunities to improve their situation and envisage a life without much in the way of excitement or reward. They are accordingly lacking in self-esteem and are generally quite hostile to the society around them, an attitude reinforced by social contact with so many young men in the same situation. Such persons exist in most urban communities, especially in grimy industrial cities where work is difficult to find. Belfast, with its 12 percent rate of unemployment and narrow gray streets of decrepit and overcrowded row houses, has more than its share of such young men. They form the rank and file of both the IRA and Loyalist para-military groups.

Communal conflict in Belfast is primarily a function of mutual fears and competition for inadequate housing and jobs. The conflict also provides a surrogate sense of purpose to young men denied expression and recognition in other more constructive forms of endeavor. Communal protection is the *raison d'etre* of Belfast's street gangs which, especially in Protestant neighborhoods, are the major social organization of the city's youths. Gang activity confers a sense of worth and belonging upon its members and permits young men, through gang exploits, to gain status among their peers. Gangs also function to transmit and harden feelings of communal exclusivity and hostility. In this sense Belfast is not unique. New York gangs, for example, function in the same manner, including their emphasis on communal warfare.

The primary difference between Belfast and other cities with major gang problems is, of course, the abnormally high level of communal tension. As a result of this tension, street gangs in working class ghettos tend to receive encouragement from powerful elements within those communities, especially from para-military organizations. In practice, the gangs teach youngsters the ways of sectarian discord. They funnel adolescents into more adult organizations which take communal violence several steps further and are responsible for most of the sectarian assassinations carried out in Belfast.

Loyalist para-military organization is difficult to describe in that it has always been highly fragmented. In addition to the already mentioned UDA, there are a myriad of other groups, among them the Ulster Volunteer Force (UVF), the Red Hand Commandos and the Loyalist Defence Association. Some of these (e.g., the Avengers) have been nothing more than short-lived cabals of a few men meeting in the backroom of a bar. Others have a large following and more formal structure. The membership of such groups has always tended to overlap.

The two most important Loyalist para-military organizations are the UVF and the UDA. There is some overlap in their membership even though relations between them, never close, have occasionally been quite violent. The UVF, the older of the two, came into being in 1966.[19] It achieved immediate notoriety when Gusty Spence and two supporters, acting in the name of the new group, gunned down four Catholics outside a bar near the Shankill Road in July of that year. Ever since, the UVF has generally been associated with the most violent brand of Loyalism.

Members of the UVF admit that "they turned to violence as a result of feelings of fear, insecurity and powerlessness" and that their military actions have been directed primarily against the Catholic community.[20] For several years prior to its 1973 cease-fire, the UVF claimed to have bombed IRA meeting places and alleged sources of finance, engaged Republican gunmen during communal confrontations and to have robbed businesses, banks and armories for funds and weapons. One brigade officer explained:

> By bombing the heart of Provisional enclaves we attempted to terrorize the nationalist community into demanding that the Provisionals either cease their campaign or move out of the ghetto areas. By bombing business premises and other such properties which we had reason to believe were terrorist meeting places or sources of revenue, we believed that we could force the Provisionals out of business, or at least cause a drastic reduction in their operational activity. By attempting to eliminate Provisional activists and "Backroom boys"—a very hard task; even for the security forces—we hoped to crack their morale and destroy their chain of command.[21]

Such a coordinated and selective campaign, as the UVF found out, required far better intelligence and more skilled cadres than it possessed. Instead, the organization increasingly began to engage in sectarian assassination, perhaps in part as a result of this failure. Although UVF leaders would not own up to it at the time, their members were responsible for many of the murders committed by Protestants through 1973. More than a dozen UVF men were actually convicted of such murders. In 1974 and 1975 they were even more active by their own admission.[22]

In November 1973 the UVF declared a cease-fire and for about a year took a very active interest in politics. The British government, attempting to encourage participation in politics as a substitute for violence, legalized the organization in April 1974. UVF leaders met with representatives of various organizations including *Sinn Fein* (Gardiner Street), the political spokesman for the Official IRA. In early 1974 UVF spokesmen went so far as to speak of working class cooperation across sectarian lines against the existing power structure of Northern Ireland.[23]

Such political pronouncements, which smacked of socialism to many Loyalists, clearly did not reflect the thinking of the rank and file and appear to have touched off a power struggle between the so-called "moderate" and "pro-Loyalist" factions. In April supporters of the more militant faction assassinated James Hanna, a member of the delegation which had traveled to Dublin for secret talks with the political representatives of the Official IRA. The Loyalist faction gained the upper hand but the flirtation with politics continued for a while and the UVF fielded candidates for local office through a political front, the hastily organized Volunteer Party. Electoral disaster prompted yet another change in leadership and a return to military activity. In response, Merlyn Rees, Secretary of State for Northern Ireland, once again proscribed the UVF in November 1975.

The exact strength of the UVF is unknown but knowledgeable sources estimate its overall membership at about 1500, with perhaps one-third of these being hard core activists. The UVF claims to be organized into seven battalions around the province. In reality, its presence is limited to Belfast, south-east Antrim (around Larne and Carrickfergus) and Portadown. Its strongest support is in West Belfast, in the lower Shankill. UVF units, even those in Belfast, appear to operate independently of each other and recognize central authority more in the breach than in practice.

The UVF speaks of itself as an elite unit claiming, for example, a much higher percentage of ex-servicemen in its ranks than other para-military groups. This assertion of professionalism must be greeted with some scepticism since security forces have always found it easier to secure convictions against the UVF than the UDA. Thus, while most observers agree that the UDA has been responsible for the lion's share of Loyalist military activity in the last few years, more UVF members have been sentenced to prison.

The UVF is also noted for its lack of cooperation with other Loyalist bodies, an attitude members describe as the result of regimental pride and others as sheer arrogance. Relations with the UDA have been especially cool and violent feuds have broken out between the two organizations on several occasions, generally over the control of local rackets.

Unlike the UVF, the UDA is an umbrella organization set up in 1972 to coordinate the activity of numerous neighborhood Loyalist groups. Authority is even more diffuse in the UDA because of the independent power bases of its constituent organizations. This decentralization has encouraged power struggles within the organization which have been accompanied by violence. Despite these internal problems the UDA can probably mobilize upwards of 20,000 men around the province, a figure that rises and falls as a barometer of Protestant feeling. These men are relatively well armed by reason of the UDA's close ties with the Ulster Defence Regiment, organized by London in 1970 to replace the discredited Special Constabulary.

The philosophy of the UDA, if one can use that term, is a rather primitive form of anti-Catholicism. Its spokesmen make no public distinction between the IRA, moderate Catholic politicians and the Catholic Church, all of whom they declare to be out to destroy Protestant liberties. Sammy Doyle, UDA press officer, asserted: "The enemy of the Ulster Protestant and the Protestant faith is the IRA Provos, aided covertly by the Roman Catholic Hierarchy. While the present violence on the part of these enemies continues the UDA will continue to carry out the function for which it was created: the defence of the Protestant people and the preservation of the Protestant faith."[24]

There is some irony to the UDA's claim that its objective is the defense of Protestants. The initial success of the UDA within the Loyalist community brought considerable power to UDA chieftans. With the erection of Protestant "no go" areas in July 1972, the UDA became the *de facto* authority in many sections of the city. Even after the barricades came down the army and RUC were reluctant to take too active a role in these neighborhoods. The UDA quickly abused its power. UDA gangs highjacked liquour lorries to supply illegal shebeens. They set up extortion rackets and sold protection to local shopkeepers and businessmen for sometimes exorbitant sums of money. Petty criminals were also forced to contribute a share of their take to UDA coffers and gradually the organization gained a near monopoly over organized crime in the Protestant sections of Belfast. While some of these excesses have been curbed by subsequent leaders, this mafia-like activity has led law abiding Loyalists to wonder if their supposed saviours were not almost as threatening as their enemies on the other side of the communal divide.

On the political front the UDA has continually pressed the British to take more strenuous action against the IRA even if this is likely to provoke violent confrontations between the army and Catholic community. In July 1972, for example, the UDA erected its own "no go" areas and declared its intention to maintain blockades in Protestant areas until the army occupied the Catholic sanctuaries in existence since the summer of 1969. This the British did on July 31 and the army-IRA clash which the UDA surely hoped to provoke failed to materialize. The organization has also participated in attempts to drive Catholics out of Protestant or mixed areas of Belfast. More recently, the UDA was one of the major organizers of the workers strike of May 1974 which brought down the Executive and effectively under-cut the British government's experiment with Catholic-Protestant power sharing in the province.

On several occasions the UDA has clashed violently with the British army, resulting in deaths on both sides. These clashes have led to a serious deterioration of army-Protestant relations similar to that which occurred in the Catholic community following earlier army-IRA confrontations. Like the IRA, the UDA has complained bitterly of army brutality. In the Shankill area, for example, UDA officers have made the same sort of allegations against the paratroopers that once came only from Catholics. They claim harassment, houses searched with frustrating frequency, members beaten, children questioned, and women insulted. The UDA would like to see the army withdrawn from Protestant streets. Since the UDA has refrained from major military operations—and probably will until the army is withdrawn—it is allowed to operate legally throughout the North.

UDA members are probably responsible for most of the sectarian assassinations carried out by the Protestant side. Often claiming to be members of the Ulster Freedom Fighters, a fictional organization invented to shield the UDA, UDA assassination squads have been active all over Belfast. The leadership of the UDA disclaims all knowledge of such activities but it is clear that they in fact encourage assassinations when it suits their purposes or at best turn a blind eye. The British Government has also chosen to ignore UDA complicity in sectarian murder for to proscribe such a powerful organization would only lead to a further deterioration of the Northern political situation.

III: The Victims

The conventional wisdom in Belfast assumes that most assassinations in that city are random sectarian killings. The available evidence does not support this conclusion. Nearly half of the murders of civilians in Belfast appear to be planned executions of specific persons.[25] Many of those killed are suspected informers or victims of leadership struggles in para-military organizations. Such people are generally killed by members of their own communal group.

Even those murders which are truly sectarian are less random than might be supposed. To begin with, almost all the victims have been men. Leaving aside deaths from bombings, only four women were assassinated up through the middle of 1973. Until quite recently, killers appeared to make conscious efforts to avoid killing women and children. There have been several instances, for example, of assassination squads accosting young couples on the street and killing the man but not molesting his date.

TABLE I
Male Assassination Victims January 1971–June 1976

Age	Number	Age	Number
14–19	30	40–44	18
20–24	21	45–49	30
25–29	16	50–54	24
30–34	19	55–59	21
35–39	13	60+	6

With respect to male victims, three-quarters of those killed (once again leaving aside deaths from bombing) were between the ages of seventeen and thirty-two. Up through June 1973 the youngest victim was fourteen and the oldest sixty-five.

The data suggest that one's chance of becoming a victim diminishes with age independently of communal affiliation.

We may speculate that the predilection for killing relatively young men is the result of several factors. Most members of para-military organizations interviewed by the author expressed revulsion at the killing of young children or the aged. Elderly people are not seen to be politically involved. Men in their prime of life by comparison are perceived as more legitimate targets for they may well be members or supporters of para-military bodies. Moreover, assassinations are generally carried out at night under the cover of darkness and neither the very young or the very old are likely to be on the street at this time.

Research suggests that victims are likely to possess a number of other defining characteristics. In almost three-quarters of the cases investigated, the victims had life styles or displayed certain forms of behavior likely to bring them to the attention of assassination squads. The most important of these characteristics are discussed below.

RESIDENCE: A significant number of victims, especially in the years 1972–1974, lived among working class members of the opposite community. Working class neighborhoods in Belfast have always been more or less segregated into Protestant and Catholic ghettos. Only a few mixed areas exist and almost all of these are middle class. Since the start of the troubles para-military organizations on both sides have sought to rigidly enforce the pattern of communal segregation. Persons who violated this social convention were highly visible and suspect. Their presence was anathema to extremists. This was especially true in Protestant ghettos. Most people who found themselves or their families to be the lone representative of their religious group in a block or entire neighborhood chose to move out or were driven out. Those who remained ran the risk of becoming victims of assassination squads and many were so warned. Such persons were attractive victims in that they could be killed with near impunity; it was not necessary for the killers to cross ethnic boundaries in search of a victim, a foray almost fraught with danger given the attempt by both communities to patrol their perimeters.

TOKEN REPRESENTATIVE AT PLACE OF WORK: The pattern of segregation in Belfast extends to employment as well, especially in working class occupations. Many firms are known to employ few or no Catholics. Harland and Wolff, the largest employer in the North, has only 400 Catholic employees out of a work force of over 10,000. Historically, the refusal of many Protestant businesses to hire Catholics can be traced to the depressed economic condition of Ulster since the 1920s. Protestant workers received preferential economic treatment in return for their loyalty to the Unionist regime.

Despite this widespread pattern of discrimination, many Catholics do work for Protestants and workers from both communities are employed by British and foreign owned firms. On the job relations between Catholic and Protestant workers are generally good although there is not likely to be any social contact between them after working hours. If anything, the odd Catholic working among Protestants has an excellent chance of becoming an assassination victim. There may be several reasons why this is the case. To begin with, the daily movements of such a worker are likely to be known to his Protestant mates. He may also cross communal boundaries to and from work. Both these characteristics make a person an easy mark. As for motive, the presence of a Catholic worker in an otherwise Protestant shop may be seen to threaten the traditional Protestant monopoly on employment or promotion, a zealously guarded prerogative given the high level of unemployment in the province. The fact that Protestant and Catholic workers can maintain good if subdued on-the-job relations may also arouse the anger of extremists.

TYPE OF EMPLOYMENT: The overwhelming majority of victims on both sides have been working class. This reflects the fact that the assassins are also working class and typically do not venture far from the safety of their own neighborhoods to carry out killings. As a result, sectarian murders have been largely confined to West Belfast, that part of the city where Protestant and Catholic working class ghettos are juxtaposed, and to the one part of East Belfast, the Short Strand, where this is also the case. However, in the course of the last year assassination squads have been ranging further afield and this has resulted in more middle class victims.

Within the working class certain kinds of occupations seem to be more hazardous than others. Service personnel who, of necessity, have daily contact with a large number of persons not necessarily known to them (e.g., shopkeepers,

off-licence proprietors, petrol station attendants) have been frequently victimized. Taxi drivers were in a particularly exposed position when the killings first began. Catholic drivers or passengers were likely to be attacked in Protestant areas and vice versa. As a result, taxi service was reorganized on a communal basis in 1971–1972. A Catholic driver, for example, will carry Catholic passengers from a central location to destinations within Catholic neighborhoods. The driver does his best to avoid Protestant areas on route. However, cabs, especially late at night, are still vulnerable to highjacking by passengers and several persons, drivers among them, have been shot in this manner.

The most dangerous profession of all is bartending. More than a dozen victims were Catholic barmen who worked in Protestant pubs or in Catholic pubs located near Protestant neighborhoods. One such shooting involved a nineteen year old barman gunned down as he emerged from work in September 1972. The Catholic bar in which he worked was in a Protestant street and the publican had previously been warned to close down. Barmen have the misfortune of working late hours and may be quite vulnerable making their way home long after closing hours. More importantly, barmen seem to have become symbolic victims. Perhaps this is because of the central role of drinking places in the social life of both communities.

OBVIOUS COMMUNAL IDENTITY: Protestants and Catholics look alike. They dress and speak alike as well. There is no obvious way of identifying the religion of most Ulstermen short of asking where they live, what school they attended or what sports they play. For this reason assassins on both sides are likely to select as victims persons whose identity is either known to them through prior association or persons whose communal identity is apparent for other reasons. Thus, any kind of street behavior which readily facilitates communal identification is foolish. Several victims, for example, were shot while walking down the street singing Republican songs. On another occasion four barmen were gunned down, according to one of the men convicted of the crime, because they had identifiable Southern accents and were thus assumed to be Catholics from the Republic.

UNACCEPTABLE SOCIAL BEHAVIOR: Dating across the communal divide is a certain way of arousing antagonism in both communities. It constitutes a flagrant rejection of sectarianism and may also arouse jealousy and resentment among the men of the community to which the woman belongs. Either reason can be sufficient to trigger a violent response. Dating a person from the other side generally also means traveling across communal boundaries given the pattern of residential segregation in Belfast. As noted earlier, this minimizes the risks for would-be assassins.

While inter-communal dating is particularly loathsome to extremists, any kind of inter-communal social activity entails some risk of reprisal as it flies in the face of attempts by extremists in both communities to foster sectarian division. A Protestant, for example, who frequents a Catholic pub is likely to get into trouble. Many of the early victims of sectarian assassins brought attention to themselves in this manner. One such incident involved a forty-one year old Protestant woman, shot to death in her house in June 1973, who had been repeatedly warmed by local UDA men to stop seeing her Catholic friends. Another case involved two young men, one Catholic and the other Protestant, killed in the Markets area, a Catholic neighborhood behind city hall. Both boys belonged to a mixed football team which had previously been warned to disband.

RISKY TRAVEL: The majority of victims are abducted or shot along communal boundaries, especially in places where Protestant and Catholic neighborhoods converge. The reasons for this are obvious. It is extremely difficult and risky for assassination squads to penetrate the heart of the other side's neighborhoods without being observed and intercepted. Making a hit on the fringes of such neighborhoods is much safer. The assassins can then make a quick get-a-way into their own territory where they are unlikely to be followed.

Certain Belfast streets have become quite notorious as the locale of numerous abductions and shootings. Among the more dangerous are Oldpark Road, the Springfield Road and the Crumlin Road. All of them are main thoroughfares which form the border between Protestant and Catholic neighborhoods. Oldpark Road, for example, the site of twenty-two abductions and murders in 1972–1973, links the Catholic Ardoyne with the Protestant Crumlin Road. The north side of Oldpark Road has traditionally been mixed and such areas, as noted earlier, are quite likely to become hotly contested as one side or the other attempts to take over by violent means.

It is wise to avoid such trouble spots, especially at night. Nevertheless, many people ignore such an obvious precaution. Almost half of the victims were shot or abducted at night while walking along roads known to be especially dangerous. For some of these people it would not have been practical to travel regularly via alternate routes given the location of their homes. For others, however, it was an unnecessary risk. Worse still, many traveled alone, further increasing their chances of ending up in the city morgue.

FOOLISH BEHAVIOR: As noted above, walking alone at night along a dangerous street is foolhardy. Other kinds of risky or foolish behavior have proven fatal. Drinking across the sectarian divide is a case in point. It cost several people their lives, among them a Protestant security guard who frequented IRA bars and was gunned down coming out of one and a Catholic taxi driver who met a similar fate in front of a Protestant bar in the Shankill. Other examples of foolish behavior include a Protestant who walked into a Catholic bar in the Short Strand and asked to join either branch of the IRA at a time when these factions were warring with each other. A known UDA man who, while drunk, accidentally wandered into a Catholic ghetto and a young Catholic photo enthusiast who attempted to cross through a Protestant district carrying his camera, also lost their lives. In 1971–1972 this kind of behavior was more understandable as there were few sectarian killings and much less public awareness as to their pattern. This is no longer true. Today, all but the most stubborn Belfast residents exercise caution in their choice of watering spots. Nevertheless, many people refuse to take other kinds of precautions and the deaths of a significant percentage of victims may still in part be attributed to careless behavior on their part.

IV: Conclusions

The prevalence and appeal of sectarian assassination will of course be influenced by a host of idiosyncratic cultural and historical conditions associated with individual cases of communal conflict. This caveat aside the Belfast experience suggests that there are certain kinds of conditions which are likely to facilitate such violence and may in fact be pre-conditions for its development.

The first of these conditions appears to be an *attitude of compliance* on the part of the assassins' community. Without such compliance assassins are unlikely to evade capture and punishment by the authorities.

Community toleration of and even support for sectarian assassination is a relatively new phenomenon in Belfast. Back in 1966 the shooting of four Catholic barmen, one of the first instances of premeditated sectarian murder, outraged people in both communities. The perpetrators, Gusty Spence and fellow members of the new UVF, were quickly brought to justice. Few gunmen are convicted today. They operate with near impunity on both sides of the sectarian divide. Gusty Spence, now dead, has become something of a folk hero for Protestant militants.

The more favorable environment in which the gunmen operate is primarily the result of the greater intensity of the struggle. This has led to greater support for extremists in both communities. Nevertheless, few Protestants or Catholics in Belfast actually condone sectarian murder. Important religious and political groups have outspokenly condemned it. Yet, there are a large number of people—perhaps a majority—who do not approve of such violence but do nothing to prevent it. For a variety of sometimes complex motives most residents of working-class neighborhoods in Belfast will not cooperate with authorities investigating sectarian murder or indeed any lawlessness originating within their community. It is this high level of tacit compliance that permits assassination gangs to operate.

There can be no doubt that much of the unwillingness to cooperate with the police in both communities is also the result of intimidation. Executions of informers and witnesses and even of vocal opponents of sectarian violence by extremist groups in both communities have deterred persons opposed to violence from stepping forward. Many residents of working class ghettos thus feel terrorized by such gangs yet powerless to do anything about it.

The degree of community control exercised by extremist groups has paralled the declining power of central authorities, the second distinguishing feature of the Belfast situation.

The police were always seen as a partisan force by the Catholic community. The B Specials, a part-time constabulary, were especially hated in this regard. The behavior of the RUC during the civil rights demonstrations of the late sixties tended to confirm the worst Catholic suspicions. In August 1969, for example, RUC men in Londonderry removed their badges and joined a drunken Protestant mob in an attack on the Catholic Bogside. In an attempt to placate Catholic opinion, London disbanded the Specials and following the imposition of direct rule made strenuous and generally successful efforts to upgrade the professional competence of the RUC. However, the Catholic community has still withheld its support of the RUC. As a result, it still remains an overwhelmingly Protestant force and does not yet patrol Catholic areas.

As noted earlier the successful Catholic defense of the Bogside in August 1969 led to the creation of "Free Derry," an internally governed area off-limits by agreement to both the police and army. Catholics set up similar "no go" areas in West Belfast as did Protestants in 1972 in an attempt to force the army to occupy the barricaded Catholic quarters. The proliferation of such independent enclaves contributed significantly to the breakdown of central authority by permitting para-military organizations from both communities to establish and extend their authority. Operation Motorman, the army's successful occupation of all no-go areas in July 1972, did little to alter this reality. Moreover, the authority of the army itself is seriously impaired by reason of its unpopularity in both communities and its obvious reluctance to become involved in a military confrontation with Loyalist forces.

The final and perhaps most important contributing condition to the escalating pattern of sectarian assassination in Northern Ireland is the existence of an apparent *political-military stalemate.* The status quo is clearly unacceptable to neither community as it leaves London holding the reins of power in the province. Yet, agreement between the communities is also out of the question as the failure of the recent constitutional convention demonstrates. The Protestant majority insists on a government representing this majority; most Catholics demand the restoration of power sharing. The inability of either side to impose a military solution or reach a political agreement only aggravates the already existing levels of frustration. This is reflected in the rising level of sectarian assassination which in 1975 became an everyday occurrence. Such violence is not likely to disappear in the absence of a political settlement. Yet, the violence, by further polarizing the two communities, diminishes the possibility of such a settlement.

NOTES

1. Martin Dillon and Denis Lehane, *Political Murder in Northern Ireland* (Harmondsworth: Penguin Books, 1973) was especially helpful as were the columns and personal assistance of Conor O'Clery and David McKitrick of *The Irish Times*. None of these journalists should be held responsible for the opinions expressed in this article, which are wholly the author's. Additional information was provided by informants within both the Royal Ulster Constabulary and the various Protestant para-military groups. For obvious reasons these sources must remain anonymous.

2. See, for example, Hannah Arendt, *On Revolution*. (New York: Viking Press, 1965); Chalmers Johnson, *Revolutionary Change*. (Boston: Little, Brown, 1966); Carl Leiden and Karl M. Schmidt, *The Politics of Violence: Revolution in the Modern World*. (Englewood Cliffs: Prentice Hall, 1968); H. L. Nieburg, *Political Violence*. (New York: St. Martin's Press, 1969); Eric R. Wolf, *Peasant Wars of the Twentieth Century*. (New York: Harper and Row, 1969).

3. See, for example, David Chalmers, *Hooded Americanism*. (New York: Doubleday, 1965); William Randel, *The Ku Klux Klan, A Century of Infamy*. (New York: Chilton, 1965); David G. Mandelbaum, *Society of India, Continuity and Change*. (Berkeley and Los Angeles: University of California Press, 1970).

4. H. Jon Rosenbaum and Peter C. Sederberg, *Vigilante Politics*. (Philadelphia: University of Pennsylvania Press, 1976), pp. 12–17.

5. See, C. Van Woodward, *The Strange Career of Jim Crow*. (New York: Oxford University Press, 1955); Morris Janowitz, "Patterns of Collective Racial Violence," in Hugh David Graham and Ted Robert Gurr, eds., *The History of Violence in America*. (New York: Bantam, 1969), p. 416.

6. Walter Schwarz, *Nigeria*. (New York: Frederick A. Praeger, 1968); John De St. Jorre, *The Brother's War: Biafra and Nigeria*. (Boston: Houghton, Mifflin, 1972).

7. For background see, Liam de Paor, *Divided Ulster*. (Harmondsworth: Penguin Books, 1972); *Northern Ireland: A Report on the Conflict*. [prepared by the *Sunday Times*] (New York: Random House, 1972); Richard Ned Lebow, "Divided Ireland," in Gregory Henderson, Richard Ned Lebow and John G. Stoessinger, eds., *Divided Nations in a Divided World*. (New York: David McKay, 1974), pp. 196–265.

8. Prior to March 1972 Northern Ireland had its own regional assembly and government responsible for the internal affairs of the province.

9. Sectarian assassinations had occurred prior to 1972 (there were five in 1971, one in 1970 and five in 1966) but not in any significant numbers.

10. For background on the IRA, see J. Bowyer Bell, *The Secret Army: The IRA, 1916–1974*. (rev.-ed., Cambridge: MIT Press, 1974), pp. 355–408.

11. Lebow, p. 221 f.f.

12. *The Irish Times*, August 26, 1975, p. 1

13. *Ibid.,* January 6, 1976, p. 1

14. Dillon and Lehane, pp. 79–80.

15. *The New York Times,* September 1, 1975, p. 9.

16. Vincent Bugliosi with Curt Gentry, *Helter Skelter: The True Story of the Manson Murders*. (New York: W. W. Norton & Co., 1974).

17. Dillon and Lehane, pp. 104–07.

18. *Ibid.,* pp. 91–96.

19. The UVF has no connection with an earlier organization of the same name organized in 1912 by Edward Carson to oppose Home Rule.

20. Interviews with UVF members; see also on anonymous article by a UVF brigade leader in the *Sunday News* (Belfast), February 3, 1974.

21. *Combat* (the newsletter of the UVF), April 19, 1974.

22. *The Irish Times*, March 18, 1975.

23. See, *Combat*, April 19, 26, 1974.

24. *The Irish Times*, February 5, 1974, p. 9.

25. Dillon and Lehane have documented this quite convincingly for murders committed prior to June 1973.

Chapter 5

MASS DESTRUCTION AND TERRORISM
Robert K. Mullen

INTRODUCTION

The concepts of mass destruction and terrorism are ancient; what is relatively recent is a frequently expressed view that terrorists will acquire the means and motivations to exercise mass destruction. This paper examines that view in terms of the means of mass destruction which exist in a technologically advanced society, what broad properties characterize such means, the resources required by a terrorist or terrorist group to implement them, and the characteristics of terrorist adversaries who may be considered potential implementers.

This is a subject frequently marked by tendentiousness, with well regarded authors sometimes adopting apocalyptic views concerning an evolution of the level of terrorism from conventional violence to mass destruction. Given that the intensity of terrorism has increased in a time in which technology is at once both more complex and more accessible, both of these factors sometimes appearing to insulate technology from the application of effective safeguards against misuse, such views are understandable, and evoke a certain sympathy.

One objective of this paper is to place the potential for mass destruction terrorism into a perspective tempered by recent and historical events relative to demonstrated terrorists' capabilities and motivations. In so doing, this discussion avoids Shultz' general category of "Establishment Terrorist,"[1] either in the sense of institutional terrorism, or terrorism applied by elements of governments, as in attempts or executions of coups d'etat. The reasons for this are several. Not the least of these is that potential mass destruction establishment terrorism is distinctly different from potential non-institutional mass destruction. Establishment terrorism in the realm of mass destruction gets into questions of treaty obligations, stability of governments, international trade in sensitive materials, and other legal, economic, and political issues which are fundamental to any discussion of potential mass destruction establishment terrorism, but which bear only tangentially on such potentials outside of legitimate governmental bodies.

This paper considers the objectives of terrorism subsumed by Shultz' general categories of Revolutionary and Sub-Revolutionary Terrorism. Nihilistic terrorism, which seems to fall outside this taxonomy, is also considered.

The capability to inflict mass destruction has until relatively recent times been limited by technology. That is to say, killing large numbers of people used to be manpower intensive: a lot of people were required to do the killing. To be sure, throwing plaque-ridden corpses over the walls of a beseiged city, or into a city's water supplies, has in the past been a tactic used to sometimes devastating effect. These are exceptions, however, and of course their occurrences represented no technological advances, nor any appreciation for the mechanisms through which mass destruction resulted.

The development and subsequent refinement of nuclear, chemical, and biological weapons has resulted in the credible possibility that a single individual could develop a capacity of causing mass destruction.[2]

Prior to addressing the potential terrorist use of mass destruction weapons, however, their characteristics are discussed in terms of the materials and active agents of which they may be composed, resources required to develop a mass destruction capability, and the problems of dissemination of the active agents of relevant weapons.

THE TERRORIST NUCLEAR THREAT
The Device

Much has been written about the availability of nuclear device design data in the open literature.[3] It is true. There appears to be sufficient material available in the unclassified literature to provide a potential bomb maker with enough information to fabricate a crude device that has some probability greater than zero of functioning in the nuclear mode. It has been estimated that such a device, containing a mass of fissionable material sufficient to produce a nuclear explosive yield of twenty kilotons (kt) TNT equivalent, could function in the range of 0.1 to 1.0 kt.[4]

The potential sources of strategic nuclear material (SNM) for the construction of a clandestine nuclear device are assumed here to be the nuclear fuel cycles for the several types of power reactors now operational. This SNM is, of course, plutonium; in particular plutonium-239 (^{239}Pu), one of several isotopes of this largely artificial element.

Although relevant, a discussion on the problems associated with recovering plutonium from spent reactor fuel, or the problems associated with overcoming safeguards designed to thwart attempts at theft or diversion of plutonium, once separated from such fuel, would perforce be a discussion of some length. Such discussion would furthermore tend to reinforce the author's conclusions. It is assumed, therefore, that the adversaries possess SNM in quantities they feel sufficient to construct a nuclear device.

Given that SNM is on hand for either direct use as core material for a clandestine nuclear device, or for conversion to a form so suitable, the additional resources required for the former include nuclear weapon design information, perhaps a small machine shop, high explosives, considerable physical and technological capability, time, space, and money. For the latter, all the above are required in addition to chemical and high temperature chemistry capabilities for conversion of the SNM to a form suitable for core construction. Depending on the nature of the basic nuclear mate-

rial on hand, it has been estimated that in some instances, a clandestine nuclear device could be constructed by a single individual.[5] Three or four individuals may constitute a more credible bomb building scenario.

Diversion of an Intact Nuclear Weapon

At first appearances, the most direct means of acquiring a private nuclear capability would seem to be through stealing an intact weapon. There are mitigating conditions, however, which even in the event of the successful acquisition of a military nuclear device, could bound the possible range of subsequent events.

A diverted military nuclear device could be used directly in a terrorist nuclear threat if the adversaries had access to appropriate resources for arming and firing the device. Arming and firing a military nuclear device frequently involves a complex series of steps in the arming procedure, and can involve also command instructions from separate firing equipment. The design purpose of any particular weapon dictates, in part, the requirements for its arming and firing. To prevent accidental or unauthorized firing, protective systems called permissive action links have been devised to increase assurance that a nuclear weapon may be armed only by following a coded sequence of events which, in some weapons, is followed by another series of events which occur during the weapon's flight to its target, and which occur independent of human control, once they are programmed.[6] Some of these permissive action links which are independent of human control, once they are programmed, include terminal velocity, barometric, or radar actuated links, as well as others.

There is another class of nuclear weapon which, although possessing permissive action links, has none of the independent permissive action links characteristic of projectile, bomb, or missile warheads. This is the atomic demolition munition (ADM); nuclear devices intended for purposes quite different from other types of nuclear munitions.[7] The ADM does, however, require a coded signal for firing. Presumably, if such a device were diverted by a clandestine group possessing the coded arming resources, such a group could go to considerable pains to acquire the firing resources as well.

Alternatively, of course, the possessor of a stolen nuclear device could attempt to bypass the arming and firing circuits. There are safeguards against such attempts, however, involving such things as disassembly of the weapon or destruction of the core's potential to become supercritical.

Superficially, it might also seem possible that the adversary could use the core of the stolen weapon in a clandestine design. This seems only marginally credible, however, since nuclear weapons are exceedingly sophisticated, being constructed in such a manner that to function in the nuclear mode it is essential the geometries of the core and the high explosive be maintained. It is essential also that the detonation characteristics of the special high explosives also be maintained. This is to say, substituting one high explosive for another in all likelihood would lead to a non-nuclear chemical explosion upon detonation of the device.

The preceding notwithstanding, there may be some efforts on the part of clandestine groups to acquire a military nuclear device. Penetration attempts have occurred at facilities where nuclear weapons are stored.[8] Unauthorized possession of a military nuclear device would be a matter of grave concern. No matter that the group possessing the device may not be able to make it function. Mere documented possession could, under some circumstances, create considerable political strain leading, in some instances, to instabilities in the ruling power structure. Cleverly implemented and manipulated, such an event could also lead to serious international problems.

In summary, the clandestinely diverted military nuclear device could be more of a threat to various power elites than to the general public, since the terrorist possession of such a weapon does not automatically imply that it is functional in such hands with one exception. Disaffected elements of the military may, under some circumstances, have control over the requisite resources to actually carry through a clandestine nuclear threat with a military nuclear device to its ultimate end. Establishment terrorism scenarios, however, are not discussed in this paper.

THE CLANDESTINE CHEMICAL OR BIOLOGICAL WEAPON
General

Chemical and biological weapons are generally perceived to be antipersonnel in nature, although there is ample evidence for the long-term area denial capacity of certain biological weapons.[9] This latter capacity, although of interest, is not germane to the principal issue of this paper, and will not be discussed further.

The antipersonnel effects of chemical and biological weapons are strongly dependent on the modes of their dissemination. This point is germinal to the relationship between the concepts of mass destruction and the potential clandestine use of chemical or biological weapons. The importance of marrying a potentially lethal agent to an adequate delivery system cannot be overestimated when the objective is mass destruction. The delivery system includes, of course, the means for getting the agent to the target area, but also includes the means for disseminating the agent once it is delivered.

The inherent differences between chemical and biological agents in their modes of action, preparation, toxicity, problems of dissemination, and other characteristics lead to a logical dichotomy, thus the characteristics of chemical and biological agents are treated serially, as are the mechanics of their preparation.

Chemical Agents

There exists a staggering array of highly toxic chemical agents. Many of these are exotic chemical formulations; others not so exotic, but relatively uncommon nevertheless. For these and other reasons, the discussion will be limited to compounds considered to be extremely toxic and which are available as byproduct, or manufacturing chemicals; chemicals employed for agricultural purposes; and chemicals of acknowledged potential utility for producing large numbers of casualties (so-called poison gases and nerve gases), for which information on chemical preparation is available in the open literature. Even with such restrictions, the list of chemical agent candidates would be unwieldly. Two artifices have been adopted to circumvent this problem. The first is to discuss classes of compounds when it is possible to do so, rather than to treat extensively individual agents within such classes. The second artifice is less elegant. It is an arbitrary choice on what to include in the discussion and what to leave out.

Another factor that has influenced the nature of the discussion of chemical agents is the relative availability in the open literature of information concerning them. There are literally tens of thousands of professional papers, monographs, and books in this literature. A trained clandestine adversary has virtually at his fingertips, at almost any university library, all the information he would need to synthesize toxic chemical agents from raw materials or intermediates.

Fluoroacetic Compounds and Their Toxic Behavior

A large number of fluoroacetic compounds have been synthesized since the original preparation of fluoroacetic acid by Swarts in 1896.[10] The toxicities of fluoroacetic acid derivatives and the potential utility of them as chemical warfare agents were not appreciated until the 1930s. Since that time, a number of more toxic derivatives have been synthesized. For those interested, practically the entire literature on fluoroacetates, to about twenty years ago, has been summarized in one book.[11] This book discusses the chemistry, preparation, toxicology, lethal doses, and other characteristics of hundreds of fluoroacetates and realted fluorine containing compounds.

Fluoroacetate compounds exert their toxic effect on living organisms by blocking essential energetic processes which preserve normal cell functions. Blockage of these processes leads to cell death and, ultimately, to the death of the organism. The speed with which these events occur after introduction of the agent into the system depends largely on relatively small differences in the chemical structures of the agents. That is, the toxicity of a parent compound may often be enhanced by making relatively minor changes in its atomic or molecular structure. Thus, fluorocarbons that differ only by one carbon atom may exhibit vastly different levels of toxicity.

There are no effective antidotes to fluoroacetate poisoning. Treatment consists of measures supportive of vital circulatory, respiratory and nervous functions. The problem appears to reside in the nature of the biochemical behavior of fluoroacetate compounds, which bind irreversibly with enzymes important in processes which supply energy to body cells.

Preparation and Utilization of Fluoroacetates and Other Fluorinated Hydrocarbons

Since there are fluoroacetate compounds available commercially, such as rodenticides, it is legitimate to ask why a terrorist, bent on mass destruction, would bother to prepare one. It would seem a simple matter to purchase or steal something like compound 1080, which is mostly sodium fluoroacetate. In fact, one cannot preclude such a possibility. However, if it is important

that there are no outward indicators of an effort to employ a clandestine chemical weapon until it is time to do so, and if the terrorist wishes to inflict a higher proportion of fatalities per unit of material disseminated than is possible with some commercially available fluoroacetates, then the preparation of a fluoroacetate may be indicated. The chemicals and equipment necessary for such preparation are easily purchased; their purchase should not arouse any suspicions concerning their ultimate use; and as suggested above, fluoroacetate compounds with much greater specific toxicity than, for example, commercial compounds based on sodium fluoroacetate, may be prepared for use in chemical weapons.

The initial steps in fluoroacetate synthesis are quite simple and straightforward, and will yield materials directly utilizable as toxic chemicals. Such processes are outlined in moderate detail in undergraduate organic chemistry text books.[12]

Fluoroacetic acid and sodium fluoroacetate have LD_{50} doses (the dose fatal to fifty percent of the exposed population) of about two to ten milligrams per kilogram of body weight (2–10 mg/kg), when ingested. On the other hand, 8-fluorooctanol, 4-fluorobutyric acid, and 8-fluorooctanoic acid have LD_{50}'s in the range of 0.6 to 0.65 mg/kg.[13] The preparation of these compounds, while somewhat more difficult than that of the simpler fluoroacetates, would present no unique challenge to a trained chemist.

One kilogram (2.2 pounds) of 8-fluorooctanoic acid contains 5,000 potentially lethal doses. A single individual could easily produce several tens of kilograms of this material in a few weeks of part-time effort. Producing a million lethal doses is largely a matter of time. Having done that, however, does not imply an ability to produce even a small fraction of that number of fatalities. The reasons why this is so are discussed later.

Organophosphorus Compounds and Their Toxic Behavior

There is a huge number of organophosphorus compounds—one estimate places the number at well over 50,000.[14] Insofar as is known, the first was synthesized around 1854. It was tetraethyl pyrophosphate, which still used as an industrial chemical known as TEPP; it is one of the most toxic of the organophosphates.

The organophosphates are in fact the most toxic of all chemical agents. Several of these are available commercially as insecticides. Parathion is one such. This particular insecticide received much publicity in the popular press due to the potential hazard it poses for agricultural workers, and due also to occasional mishandling which led to fatalities such as happened in Tijuana, Mexico, some years ago when this agent was stored in a mill and contaminated flour which was subsequently consumed as bread.

Between the world wars, the synthesis of organophosphorous compounds for insecticidal purposes was pursued in Germany. In the mid-1930s, the general formula for these was patented as a contact insecticide. In accordance with the law as it then existed in Germany, all new toxic chemicals were to be submitted to the government for examination as possible agents of war. The organophosphates were thus quickly adopted by the military. Tabun and Sarin, compounds developed by the private chemical industry in Germany while investigating the insecticidal potentials of the organophosphates, were incoporated into the German military armamentarium.

Another organophosphate, diisopropyl fluorophosphate (DFP), was synthesized in the U.S. in the early 1940s and it found considerable use among biochemists who have used it as a taggant in mapping many biochemical and metabolic processes, especially those involved in certain enzymatic reactions. Although it is a poison—relatively mild by standards to be considered here—DFP has been produced in a clandestine laboratory for what would appear to be assassination purposes.[15]

A huge open literature on organophosphates exists in part due to military interest, but also because of interest in commercial and academic circles concerning the chemistry of this family of compounds which has considerable economic importance as insecticides, and because of interest which developed in the 1950s in basic research on nerve activity, in particular the electrochemical transmission of nerve signals, and the action of the enzyme acetylcholinesterase—an enzyme involved in the electrochemical phenomena which transmit signals from one nerve ending to another. Organophosphorous compounds block the action of acetylcholinesterase, interrupting the transmission of signals along nerve pathways.

As mentioned prevously, the family of organophosphate compounds contains within it the most toxic of all chemicals. They are lethal, albeit in different specific weights, whether administered orally, whether they are respired, or whether they came into contact with the skin. It is said that in the past, careless crop dusters who allowed liquid Parathion to splash on their shoes died when the liquid penetrated the leather of their footwear and came into contact with the skin of their feet. Such tales may be apocryphal, but the toxicity of some of the organophosphates is impressive. It is known, for example, that extremely small droplets of some of these compounds, when they come in contact with the eye, are fatal.[16]

The toxicity of the previously discussed fluoroacetate compounds was expressed in terms of oral doses to humans. The picture is somewhat more complex when discussing the toxicity of organophosphates, however, since there are such a variety of them; their toxicities vary over one or two orders of magnitude depending on the species tested and route by which administered; chemical purity of the compound may be difficult to establish with certainty; and other factors that tend to make the toxicity issue somewhat less straightforward than that for fluoroacetates.

The LD_{50} for TEPP by the oral route is stated by Heath[17] to be in the range of 1.05 to 1.70 mg/kg, and by another authority, 2.4 to 7.0 mg/kg,[18] when applied on the skin. On the other hand, the oral LD_{50} for Sarin is in the range of 0.14 to 0.28 mg/kg.[19] Sarin is highly volatile, which may explain its relatively low skin dose toxicity as compared to TEPP (about 17 mg/kg.)[20] This high volatility leads to some rather bizarre effects, however. Among these is that a very small quantity of Sarin dropped on the skin is likely to lead to a vapor concentration in the vicinity of the person on whom the Sarin was dropped which exceeds the LD_{50} inhalation dose for a single breath! That dose can be worked out from figures in one authoritative publication,[21] which indicates that the inhalation LD_{50} dose is 75 mg/min/m³ (75 mg Sarin per cubic meter of air per minute). At normal respiratory rates, this is an LD_{50} dose of about 0.015 mg/kg.

Still more potent organophosphates are found in that group of agents commonly referred to as V-agents. The generic formula for the V-agents is widely known, and is:

$$R - P(O) \begin{matrix} OR' \\ SCH_2CH_2NR''_2 \end{matrix}$$

where the substituents R, R' and R'' are, in general, short chain aliphatics (non-aromatic hydrocarbons with 2–4 carbon atoms).[22] The agent VX is in this family, and its formula is regarded as secret, although it, and its method of preparation, has been published by the British Patent Office. Enough information has appeared also in the U.S. press to deduce both the formula and the preparatory routes to its manufacture.[23]

The toxicity of VX by the respiratory route is estimated to be approximately 15 times that of Sarin,[24] or about 0.001 mg/kg. VX is relatively non-volatile as well, and it has been stated that 6 mg applied to the skin is lethal; which makes VX about 300 times more lethal than Sarin by this route.[25]

These figures should be taken as relative toxicities only. Even then, relationships between toxicities of different agents are difficult to quantify for a number of reasons, some of which were outlined previously. The important point to recognize is that the organophosphates which have been selected, studied, and stockpiled by various nations as chemical weapons, and which are in use world-wide as insecticides, are among the most toxic synthetic agents developed by man.

Death can come from a variety of causes resulting from the action of an organophosphate, and descriptions of the symptoms predisposing to death are not important here. Death from organophosphate poisoning may be so rapid that the afflicted individual may be entirely unaware of what is happening.

*Preparation and Utilization of
Organophosphate Compounds*

A perpetrator of a mass destruction event, whose vehicle were to be an organophosphate could: (1) acquire a compound directly through commercial channels; or (2) explosively rupture a vehicle transporting such a compound. It is a credible thesis that an event of high consequence could be precipitated, or threatened, by explosively dispersing such an agent in an appropriate environment, or by stealing a truckload of it for purposes of extortion. Of course, the latter threat could be credibly precipitated with much less than a truckload quantity.

Organophosphates which are less common or absent from normal commercial channels, could be manufactured in a clandestine laboratory. The greater the toxicity of the agent, of course, the less

material may be required to accomplish the intended end.

For example, Sarin can be synthesized in a small laboratory in quantities sufficient to cause thousands of deaths, presuming efficient dispersal of the agent, for a modest investment in chemicals and laboratory supplies. The starting chemicals are available commercially, syntheses processes are in the open literature, and the appropriate laboratory ware available from almost any laboratory supply house. The preparative schemes (and there are several) for synthesizing 100g quantities of Sarin could be considered tedious; they do involve hydrofluoric acid, a difficult acid to handle, but these procedures are well within the capabilities of an organic chemist with some graduate training.[26] As, it may be added, are the procedures for the synthesis of Tabun,[27] an organophosphate more toxic than Sarin.

A variety of V-agents may be prepared with somewhat more difficulty than that required to manufacture Sarin. More steps are involved; the procedure more hazardous due to the nature of some of the intermediate products and the final product, but again the processes are well within the capabilities of a graduate chemist.[28]

The utility of the organophosphates as instruments of mass destruction would appear to be obvious. They would appear to possess, on a weight-for-weight basis, an inherent advantage over the fluoroacetates in their capacity to cause fatalities. On balance, that is indeed the case. There are, however, so many variables associated with effective delivery of a chemical for mass destruction purposes, as to make a straightforward comparison between the potential lethalities of fluoroacetates and organophosphates a most difficult proposition.

BIOLOGICAL AGENTS
General

There are some differences between biological and chemical agents which go beyond basic differences between living systems, or their products, and synthetic ones. For example, one may discuss chemical agents by whole categories, or families, if you will. Witness the previous remarks on fluoroacetates and organophosphates. Both are natural groups of chemicals and both contain thousands to tens of thousands of chemicals within each.

When discussing potential biological agents, however, the discussion is usually limited to a specific organism, or product of that organism. This is not quite true since there are different serological types of an organism which, for purposes of arranging in a systematic hierarchy, taxonomists may refer to as a single species. For example, six serological types of *Clostridium botulinum*, the bacterium which produces botulinum toxin, are known, but taxonomists recognize only the one species. (There are other species of *Clostridium*, of course, but that is not relevant to this point.)

There are also different strains, subspecies, or species, of particular genera of organisms which exhibit varying levels of toxicity. *Bacillus anthracis*, for example, is one of the most poisonous organisms known. Another species of *Bacillis, B. cereus*, is on the other hand quite harmless.

Biological agents are therefore discussed on individual species bases and not on the basis of properties shared in common with a large number of kindred compounds, as is possible with some chemical agents.

Botulinum Toxin and Its Toxic Behavior

Botulinum toxin is a neurotoxin produced by *Clostridium botulinum*, and is among the most poisonous of toxins known. One may argue whether it is more properly discussed under chemicals or biologicals, since it is not a living entity but is a toxin produced by a living organism. Since it is a natural product of the metabolism of a living organism, however, and not a synthetic chemical, I have elected to discuss it with the biologicals.

Botulinum toxin, of course, causes botulism. What may be less well appreciated, however, is the fact that while 5–10 milligrams or so of a V-agent, the most potent of the synthetic chemical agents of mass destruction, may be required to cause a human fatality, a few micrograms of botulinum toxin will do the same thing. In short, botulinum toxin is about a thousand times more toxic than the organophosphates, and a million times more toxic than any fluoroacetate.

With respect to the mechanisms of action of botulinum toxin; those mechanisms are not known in the detail that those of the fluoroacetates or organophosphates are known. Even the human LD_{50} for botulinum toxin is not precisely known. It is assumed to lie somewhere between less than a microgram (a millionth of a gram) and a few micrograms. One of the prob-

lems inherent in determining human LD_{50} doses for such small amounts of material is the fact that the amounts are so small. This in itself makes any quantitative assay, on a postmortem examination for example, virtually impossible. Further complicating that job is the chance that the victim ingested not only botulinum toxin, but live botulinum bacilli as well, which go on producing toxin in the body of the victim.

Extrapolation of the human LD_{50} dose from animal experimentation is not possible either, because of the peculiar manner in which various non-primate species respond to this agent. Some species respond in a straightforward manner in which the LD_{50} dose is a function of body weight; i.e., the heavier the animal, the greater the LD_{50} dose. In other species the LD_{50} dose may be independent of body weight. Figures for human LD_{50} doses by inhalation are published, however,[29] and correspond to a total LD_{50} dose to the human of about 0.3 micrograms, or about 5000 times more toxic than the organophosphate Sarin.

Like the organophosphates, botulinum toxin acts on the nervous system. Botulinum toxin blocks the transmission of nerve impulses, as opposed to the organophosphate action of preventing those impulses from being turned off.

This is, essentially, the state of knowledge today concerning the mechanisms of action of botulinum toxin. The victim of botulinum toxin poisoning, should that victim succumb, succumbs frequently to paralyses of the respiratory muscles—the victim suffocates.[30]

Preparation and Utilization of Botulinum Toxin

Clostridium botulinum, the bacillus which produces botulinum toxin, is found in soil virtually everywhere. One may, from a trowel full of dirt, culture *C. botulinum*. To be assured of getting a virulent form of *C. botulinum*, however, a bit more sophistication is required.

Botulism is, of course, an ever-present danger to the food industry. For that reason, public health agencies and the medical profession in general have long studied *C. botulinum*, developing procedures for isolating and culturing various species of clostridia (some clostridia cause gangrene or tetanus). Because of this interest, the open literature has long contained detailed descriptions of the isolation, culturing, and testing of species of *Clostridium*.[31]

A terrorist interested in preparing a culture of *C. botulinum* for purposes of extracting botulinum toxin could attempt to grow the organism rather than try to obtain a culture of it from, say, the American Type Culture Collection. Growing your own requires a certain amount of screening for the proper serologic type; assuming a terrorist would wish to maximize the lethality of a toxin, it is necessary that his *C. botulinum* be tested for serologic type. The processes for doing this are somewhat involved if the terrorist is insistent on maximum security, precluding the purchase of standardized anti-toxins for serologic typing: involved, but not unmanageable for the trained individual.

Once the proper serologic type of *C. botulinum* is identified, it may be isolated and grown under anaerobic conditions in pure culture, from which continuous production of toxin is possible. It may be desirable to purify and concentrate this product. Directions for doing so are in the open literature. With modest facilities, an individual could produce in a relatively short period several hundred thousand human LD_{50} doses of botulinum toxin.

There are risks associated with these procedures; self-contamination is possible if special precautions are not taken. It may be assumed, however, that an individual with the capability to prepare botulinum toxin is well aware of the health and safety risks involved, and will have taken appropriate steps to eliminate those risks.

The product may be of unknown toxicity, but in any case, could be a most toxic agent. The utility of botulinum toxin as an agent of mass destruction is enhanced by the fact it is highly toxic by inhalation or ingestion. Ultimately, however, as with all agents of mass destruction discussed in this paper, its utility for mass destruction purposes depends for the most part on an effective means of dissemination.

Anthrax and Its Toxic Properties

We are now into discussing an agent which is clearly and unambiguously biological. This agent is a living organism—not a toxin produced from it. Furthermore, this agent is perhaps the most toxic substance within the capabilities of a terrorist to employ.

Anthrax bacilli are highly infective, particularly potent casualty producers, resistant in spore form to environmental factors of heat, moisture, cold and dessication. The bacillus occurs in cutaneous, intestinal, and respiratory forms.

A particularly insidious quality of anthrax

poisoning is the fact that it must be treated before it is obvious what disease the patient has in order that a modest chance for survival can exist. Waiting to provide treatment until the symptoms are obvious virtually guarantees the patient will die within two to three days. It is sobering to note that even at Fort Detrick, where more elaborate safety measures were in force than in any other comparable facility in the U.S. (one may argue there was no other facility comparable to Fort Detrick when it was engaged in the production and investigation of biological agents), two employees died of anthrax in the late 1950s.[32] In its respiratory form, anthrax is frequently fatal within twenty-four hours.

The infectious mechanisms of anthrax are relatively well understood; however, the mechanisms through which toxicity is mediated are not well in hand. Along this line, if certain chemicals are mixed with anthrax spores and the mixture administered in concentrations which are not lethal when either the chemical or anthrax is administered singly, anthrax infections are nevertheless produced. Just why such synergism is displayed in these cases is not well understood.

The toxicity of *B. anthracis* seems to be mediated through a chemical factor produced by the bacillus which overwhelms defense mechanisms the body normally arrays against infections. The vegetative growth and reproduction of infective bacilli progress relatively unimpeded throughout the respiratory tract; the lymphatic and blood circulatory systems are rapidly invaded; and the infection widely disseminated to other organs throughout the body. The infection proceeds with uncommon speed, and death in 24 hours or less is not unusual. Although a number of vaccines are available, unless the disease is recognized very early, the utility of these vaccines for reducing mortality is minimal.

Preparation and Utilization of Anthrax

Bacillus anthracis, like *Clostridium botulinum,* can be prepared in continuous culture. Prior to such preparation however, a seed culture must be obtained. This should present only moderate difficulty to virtually anyone with a background in microbiology or a related discipline. University and public health research laboratories, pharmaceutical research laboratories, and other sources exist where a seed culture could be obtained under apparently legitimate circumstances. For maximum security, the terrorist may choose to acquire his seed culture from the natural environment in which *B. anthracis* lives. Procedures for sampling, screening, identifying, isolating, and culturing almost any biological organism of public health concern are published widely in microbiological texts and manuals, the sampling, care, and feeding of *B. anthracis* included. This organism would appear to be a good choice for a potential mass destruction weapon: once it is obtained in seed culture it grows rapidly and requires only moderate care, and readily forms spores.

Once a terrorist has obtained a seed culture, the organism may be grown in quantity by either continuous culture methods, or in batches. Again, generic directions for doing so are freely accessible in the open literature. Methods of mass culture of organisms closely related to *B. anthracis* (*B. cereus* and *B. subtilis*) have been discussed[33] and could be used by a terrorist to perfect techniques before attempting mass culture of the anthrax bacillus.

A terrorist has a number of options available for isolation and concentration of *B. anthracis* from the culture medium. Simple centrifugation will separate the cells from the culture medium, which can then be suspended in a stabilizing medium and stored under refrigeration. Virulence of the stored cells could be maintained under such conditions for several weeks. Alternatively, it may be desired to maintain stocks in spore form, in which case the organism would be permitted to sporulate, then separated from culture, dried, and stored in the dark. Virulence could be maintained for years under these conditions.

Dispersal of deadly chemical or biological agents is frequently treated in the popular press as no more difficult than dumping the agent in a community water supply. So done, mass casualties are deduced to automatically result. Rarely could this be the case, however. The efficient dispersal of a potential agent of mass destruction could be a formidable problem for anyone contemplating such an act. Some of the difficulties associated with efficient dispersal of a toxic agent are discussed in the following section.

DISPERSAL OF TOXIC AGENTS
Chemical Agents

In previous sections addressing the preparation and utilization of chemical agents, it was implied that relatively large quantities of materials could be produced with only moderate requirements. In general, this is true. It also can be misleading,

however, to assume that a given quantity of agent is translatable to a capability to produce some number of deaths with that quantity. For example, if the objective of an individual were to produce, say 5,000–10,000 casualties, depending on the method of dispersal chosen, up to one million times this amount in LD_{50} doses may have to be produced. No matter what route of agent dissemination is chosen, losses during dissemination will occur. These losses are usually quite large: at a minimum, it may be assumed that 90 percent of the dispersed agent will not reach the intended target in doses sufficient to cause casualties. This is a very general statement, of course, and if the adversary were judicious in choice of target and method of dispersal, losses could perhaps be reduced.

Several methods of dispersing chemical agents may be considered. These include contamination of bulk food supplies; generation of gases in enclosed spaces with volatile agents; generation of aerosols in enclosed spaces with non-volatile agents; and dispersal with explosives.

The first three of these dispersal mechanisms are assumed would occur under covert conditions; the last, overtly. The number of scenarios for dispersal is virtually limitless. It is, however, doubtful that an adversary could under any conditions, with a high probability effectively target a group of people larger than a few hundred with any kind of chemical attack. If an adversary were to attempt an attack on a larger scale, such an attempt would likely be made out of ignorance concerning the logistical, dispersal, and material resources required to launch such an attack effectively. These requirements place the chemical mass destruction attack in the realm of a very large scale undertaking which, for a number of reasons, is not considered credible.

On the other hand, an attack with chemical agents on a select population of individuals, such as the inhabitants of an office building or large auditorium, is an attack which is manageable by a single individual. Whether one would characterize the result of such an attack as mass destruction is largely a matter of how one defines that term. Peacetime man-caused disasters (fires, explosions, etc.) that result in a hundred fatalities or more are quite rare. An event involving a chemical agent attack on a select population which resulted in several hundred deaths would be a significant event indeed, with effects extending far beyond the immediate tragedy. Although the clandestine chemical attack does not appear a viable method for producing very large numbers of fatalities, an event which resulted in a few hundred fatalities could certainly be categorized as an event of mass destruction.

Biological Agents

With the exception of botulinum toxin, the effective dispersal of biological agents is for the most part limited to aerosolization. Aerosols are, of course, suspensions of small particles in a gaseous medium. Not all aerosols that could be made up of pathogenic or toxic particles would, by the nature of their constituents, be necessarily harmful, however. That is largely due to the fact that the possible particle size range of an aerosol is rather broad, while the particle size range of aerosols which will effectively involve the human respiratory system is relatively limited.

This is a very simplistic explanation of the relationships of aerosol particles to the human respiratory system, and it is for the most part more appropriate to a discussion of non-living aerosol particles than to a discussion of living particles. (See the discussion on plutonium dispersal.) Aerosols made up of a virulent organism such as B. anthracis may be somewhat effective even if particle sizes are outside the range of those most effectively trapped by the respiratory system. The residence time of too small or too large particles (i.e., the time to clear these particles from the respiratory system) may be sufficient to permit their toxic factors to be released, or for the spores making up the particles to reproduce. Furthermore, particles cleared from the respiratory tree may be swallowed. B. anthracis is also toxic if the intestinal form is ingested.

A significant problem in the aerosol dissemination of almost any biological agent, is the survival of the agent long enough to infect the intended target. The mechanical stresses in the aerosolization process may kill a significant proportion of the pathogenic agent. Moisture in the air, sunlight, smog, radical temperature changes, and other factors may contribute to reducing, through death of significant numbers of organisms in the agent, the virulence of that agent. Thus, as with chemical agents, it is misleading to equate the number of LD_{50} doses an adversary may possess with the number of LD_{50} doses delivered, irrespective of a host of other problems associated with aerosol delivery, others of which are touched upon later with respect to the discussion on pluto-

nium.

It is not in the objectives of this paper to go in depth into methods of aerosol delivery. No purpose would seem to be served by doing that. Suffice it to say that if an adversary possessed some basic understanding of meteorology, the biological characteristics of the agent he chose to employ, the requirements for and affects of aerosolization, was careful in the selection of the target population, and was aware of the various temporal and spatial conditions which would affect the aerosol dispersal of a particular organism, a significant threat could arise. That adversary could precipitate an event which, by anyone's definition, would be an event of mass destruction.

Recall further that spores of B. anthracis are quite resistant to many environmental factors. To illustrate, the Island of Gruinard off the coast of Scotland was used by the British in World War II for testing biological weapons. Anthrax was tested there, and it was estimated in 1967 that the island may remain infected with viable anthrax for one hundred years.[34]

To summarize, there appear no technological impediments to the mounting of a credible clandestine mass destruction threat with some biologicals; such would appear more difficult with potential chemical agents. The resources required to mount a credible mass destruction threat with a biological weapon are trivial compared to those required for a credible explosive nuclear threat.[35] A similar statement could be made for the nuclear compared to the chemical threat, but by any measure, it does not seem credible that a chemical threat could be mounted that could result in the magnitude of destruction potentially possible with nuclear or biological weapons.

It should not be assumed from the above that any value judgment is being made with respect to the mounting of any mass destruction threat. This is quite a separate question.

THE PLUTONIUM DISPERSAL WEAPON—A SPECIAL CASE

As implied earlier, the apparent simplicity of the aerosol device, in one form or another of ubiquitous household familiarity, has seemingly led to the assumption that aerosols themselves are easy to produce. Which in fact they are, relatively speaking, but uncritical acceptance of this tends to lead also to the assumption that effectively toxic aerosols of plutonium are also easy to produce.

The following observations on the toxic properties of plutonium are presented with a view towards placing the issue of plutonium dispersal, as employed in a radiological weapon, into some perspective. Since inhalation is the most sensitive route of entry into the body relative to the toxicity of plutonium, other modes of entry (ingestion or accidental injection) are not discussed.

Particles of small enough dimensions, and in large enough density in space and time to be classed as aerosols, possess a number of interesting characteristics which, in the past and current debates concerning the relationship of plutonium to some usually poorly defined capability to cause death or injury when introduced into the respiratory system, have by and large been ignored. There are, of course, scholarly exceptions to this generalization;[36] but these also seem to be ignored in present debate. The reasons for this are not altogether clear, since many of the principles required to perform adequate assessments of the behavior of aerosols in the atmosphere, in the respiratory system, and the expected toxicity of plutonium aerosols in particular, are relatively well in hand.

Aerosol particles behave differently in a relatively free aerodynamic environment, as in the atmosphere, than they do in the aerodynamic environment of the respiratory tree. It is important to possess at least a basic understanding of the behavior of aerosol particles in both environments before one can say much that is credible concerning the potential toxicity of a plutonium aerosol.

Producing an aerosol may be by one of several means. Aerosols may be generated aerodynamically, by centrifugal action, hydraulically, by vibration, or through electrostatic processes. The aerodynamic method is the most common. Here, however, a distinction must be made concerning the material from which the aerosol is generated. Aerodynamic generation of an aerosol from a liquid as, for example, from hydrated plutonium nitrate, involves forcing the liquid with high pressure air through a nozzle or other terminal device which breaks up the liquid into small particulates of the desired size. If, however, the starting material is solid as, for example, plutonium dioxide powder or plutonium nitrate crystals, the particulates must first be formed mechanically. Once formed, the particles are then propelled by air pressure (or some other gas) through an air pipe, hose, or some other delivery device.

Once the aerosol is formed, its behavior in the atmosphere is affected by processes which operate to greater or lesser degree to degrade the presumed desired performance of the aerosol.

In an external environment, effective distribution of an aerosol depends upon the height from which it is released, local air currents, density of suspended particles at an effective height for an effective period of time, particle size, and amount of starting material. These factors, and those mentioned previously, may provide some indication of the problems facing any terrorist who would disperse a plutonium aerosol in the open environment with the objective of causing large numbers of short-term fatalities.

Effective dispersal of a plutonium aerosol indoors is not without its problems either. It is generally accepted that the most efficient manner in which to disperse a plutonium aerosol into a building is via the air conditioning system. Frequently implicit in such scenarios is perfect mixing and ideal aerosol cloud stability within the building, since rarely does one ever find discussed any of the problems inherent in such a scenario. These include plating out of a significant proportion of the aerosol particles on the enormous surface areas of the air conditioning duct work of large buildings; the effect of air conditioning, especially humidification, on the aerosol particles; the effects of passive and electrostatic filters on the aerosol; and other factors, including many of those previously discussed, which in general would act to degrade the desired performance of a plutonium aerosol introduced into a building's air conditioning system.

Up to this point, no mention has been made of the dependency for effectiveness of a plutonium aerosol on the particle size distribution of that aerosol, i.e., the relationship between particle sizes and the characteristics of respiratory physiology. As a general statement it may be said that up to 25 percent of the particles inhaled from an aerosol, which are in the size range of 0.5 microns (millionths of a meter) to about 7 microns, will be deposited in deep lung tissue. Above 7 microns, the proportion of particles deposited in deep lung tissue declines sharply. Particles of less than 0.5 microns may be phagocytized (engulfed by cells specialized for removing foreign material), or actually move through the interstitial spaces between cells, and migrate out of the lungs.

Particle sizes of plutonium compounds found in nuclear facilities frequently fall within the respiratory size range, although particle sizes of plutonium in fuels for experimental reactors may be 2–3 times larger than the upper range indicated here.[37]

Before relating this information to the respiratory physiology of aerosol particles in general, and plutonium in particular, it is necessary to describe in a superficial manner the structure and characteristics of the respiratory system relative to particle deposition. For present needs, it is sufficient to divide this system into three zones: the nasopharyngeal, the tracheobronchial, and the pulmonary. The nasopharyngeal zone consists of the nose and that portion of the airway to the level of the trachea. This zone of the respiratory system will entrap approximately 80 percent of inhaled aerosol particles up to 7 microns in aerodynamic diameter, and larger yet proportions of particles above this size. These particles, after entrapment, are cleared from this zone in one-half times of a few hours to one or two days.

The tracheobronchial zone includes the airway from the trachea, through the bronchus and bronchi, to and including the terminal bronchioles. Some small fraction of aerosol particles are deposited in this zone by impaction, sedimentation, or diffusion in the case of very small particles. An anatomical feature of this zone is that it is both ciliated and contains mucous-secreting glands, which together clear the zone of deposited foreign particles in one-half times of 30 minutes to about one day, depending on particle size, point of deposition, and health of the individual.

The pulmonary zone is where functional gas exchange takes place in the lungs, and structurally consists of small sacs termed alveoli. Very few particles deposited in the alveoli exceed 7 microns in aerodynamic diameter. Residence one-half times in this zone can be long for insoluble particles, such as plutonium dioxide, and are frequently assumed to be on the order of 500 days.[38] One must say assumed, because clearance mechanisms from this zone are not completely understood. As might be expected, the pulmonary zone is the sensitive target area for a plutonium aerosol. It is in the pulmonary zone where pathological conditions induced by a plutonium aerosol can cause fatalities, given that enough material is deposited.

Which gets us, finally, to the question of plutonium toxicity. This issue has been confused by attempting to equate the toxicity of plutonium with a lethal substance such as nerve gas. It is a poor comparison, since nerve gases do not have to be inhaled or ingested to be lethal. Sarin, as previously noted a potent nerve gas, has gained a certain amount of popularity in terms of comparable toxicity vis-à-vis plutonium. It is lethal in milligram quantities. Under some conditions, a milligram or two dropped on the clothing, and soaking through to the skin where it may be absorbed, is a lethal dose. Microgram quantities striking the eye are lethal. On the other hand, a milligram or two of a plutonium aerosol, applied to external body surfaces only, is completely innocuous, as is a kilogram or two applied in the same manner. One may wish to make a distinction at this point between the radiobiological effectiveness of weapons grade plutonium versus reactor grade plutonium, but the distinction in this context would be academic.

The toxicity of plutonium, or any other material for that matter, is expressed in terms of some minimum amount which has some probability of causing a pathological effect. In the case of plutonium, as mentioned previously, this is a function of the mode of entry into the body, which is not true to the same extent of some other toxic substances. Selecting the most sensitive route of entry, through the respiratory system, plutonium toxicity becomes expressable in terms of that quantity of material, deposited in the pulmonary region of the respiratory system, that has a high probability of leading to short-term (one year, or less) fatalities. Experimentation on dogs indicates that this quantity, for insoluble plutonium, is about five billionths of a curie per gram of lung tissue. Death arises from pulmonary fibrosis.[39]

Making some extremely simplistic calculations, and extrapolating directly from the animal data, it may be shown that milligram quantities of insoluble reactor grade plutonium, deposited in the pulmonary region of the human lung, will cause a short-term fatality in that individual so exposed. Such calculations do not, however, take into consideration any of the previously mentioned physical factors which tend to degrade the performance of any aerosol; the environmental factors which affect the time and space occupancy characteristics of any aerosol; the physiological factors which require an aerosol to possess certain characteristics if it is to be effective; and other factors which make any attempt to cause numbers of short-term fatalities from a plutonium aerosol, an undertaking of great uncertainty.

Which is to say, calculations indicating milligram quantities of insoluble reactor grade plutonium are lethal are based upon data obtained on laboratory animals in strictly controlled environments, and under exposure conditions which ensured the pulmonary deposition of controlled quantities of plutonium oxide. One must recognize that any relationship between such environments, designed specifically to result in pulmonary depositions of aerosol particulates, and virtually any other environment into which an aerosol may be dispersed, is tenuous in the extreme.

Frequently seen statements that small quantities of plutonium, dispersed into undefined environments, in some undefined manner, and made without consideration of the problems involved in creating an aerosol, much less those of maintaining its integrity once discharged from the aerosol generator, causing thousands of deaths, are simply incredible.

If it were possible to confine one thousand people to a controlled environment in which each individual was, through a breathing apparatus specially constructed for the purpose, separately administered about one milligram of reactor grade plutonium oxide, it would only require about one gram of such material to cause short-term mortality in that population of individuals. Under any other conditions, the dispersal of an aerosol of reactor grade plutonium oxide, done with the objective of causing one thousand or so short-term fatalities, would have to be a brute force operation.

It is difficult to argue against the proposition that to cause one thousand short-term fatalities from the inhalation of an aerosol of reactor grade plutonium, it would require material in amounts up to a million times greater than that required to accomplish the same thing in a controlled environment such as that just outlined. That is, it would require some amount of material in the range of 1,000 kilograms, or one metric ton, to attempt the feat, and the outcome would still be uncertain because of the many factors which operate on all aerosols, and over which no control is possible. Conditions for dispersal may be selected to optimize the opportunity to create greater hazards, of course. There remain many variables, however, over which manipulation is possible only in a probabilistic sense. Thus, the outcome of

a brute force plutonium aerosol attack of even incredible proportions could not be predicted with certainty.

In sum, the "poison gas" characterization of a plutonium aerosol must be put into a perspective appropriate to certain unavoidable physical and physiological prerequisites for the application of such material in a manner designed to cause short-term fatalities. In that regard, it may be useful to consider the fact that to have some probability of success in causing thousands of casualties in a military operation, even so-called nerve gas gases must be dispersed in quantities of hundreds to thousands of kilograms.

The plutonium dispersal weapon is, simply, not a weapon of mass destruction. This is not to minimize the other characteristics of such a weapon which include radiological contamination and the potential for causing life-shortening through induction of cancers in individuals 15 to 30 years following exposure. This is a separate subject, however, and one which also has seemed to suffer more than benefited from much of recent discussion.

MASS DESTRUCTION AND TERRORISM

This subject, among many other things, requires transcultural evaluations of motivational stimuli. In some instances such evaluations simply may not be possible. Motivation, as an aspect of modern human behavior, is increasingly difficult to assess in the traditional terms of an advanced industrial Western society. To the Western mind, recent terrorist acts frequently seem irrational.

The problem of assessing in rational Western terms the political and/or sociological aspects of a terrorist mass destruction threat is further complicated by the fact that such a threat is an extraordinary act: this kind of threat involves skills, values, and risks that are not encountered in more conventional forms of terrorism. Extrapolations of past terrorist activities to encompass the terrorist employment of a weapon of mass destruction may be misleading. Which is not to say that past terrorist activity should not be examined in an attempt to evaluate the motives leading to the consummation of such a threat. For better or worse, this past and continuing activity represents the only reservoir of human experience from which it is possible to develop a qualitative assessment of factors which could be predisposing to a mass destruction threat.

In the popular press, learned journals, books,

and monographs, the potential relationship between terrorism, as it is increasingly practiced around the world, and a terrorist mass destruction capability has received considerable attention; particularly with regard to a potential nuclear threat. Analyses of terrorism found in the popular press often state that terrorists will ultimately acquire a nuclear capability (from civilian or military sources), and then be in a position to wield extraordinary powers of extortion or political blackmail.[40] Similar sentiments have been expressed in more learned works.[41] Recently, however, the assumptions that terrorists would acquire means for inflicting mass destruction as a natural evolutionary sequence have been attacked, largely on the basis of analyses of the raison d'etre of terrorist movements.[42]

There is no question that, under appropriate circumstances, terror has proven to be both an effective and efficient psychological weapon. No other technique is as immediately available or offers as much return for relatively small investments as does selectively applied terror. Conditions are important, however, and, as Simpson puts it:

> . . . the competent practitioners of terrorism usually know how their actions will affect their enemies and what reactions they can expect from those not directly involved.[43]

Implied in Simpson's remark is the requirement that there be limitations to any terror campaign. Most authorities agree that non-institutional terrorism is a tactic of the weak. This being the case, in order for terror to be an effective tactic for coercion, terrorists must be able to make their constituencies understand what is being attempted, and let them know that there are penalties involved and that innocents will be spared to the degree possible.[44] The use of weapons of mass destruction could violate each of these criteria. Such weapons could kill or injure innocent people in very large numbers; the penalties would far exceed any accepted norms for conventional violence; and the terrorist message would likely be lost in the revulsion engendered by any such attack.

The recent shift in perspective—from perceiving terrorist movements as naturally progressing to a mass destruction, and in particular nuclear capability, to a more measured appraisal of those movements—has revealed some analytical superficialities in the earlier literature. Only recently have there been attempts to reexamine terrorist movements in terms of ultimate goals and objectives, insofar as employment of weapons of mass destruction within these movements is concerned. For example, a recent exhaustive search of the literature dealing with Arab terrorist fedayeen, which is replete with references to non-nuclear military and guerrilla strategies, has revealed only one reference to the possible fedayeen use of nuclear explosives. This reference arose in an interview with a Western scientist who discussed the potential ease of manufacture of a clandestine nuclear device.[45]

Historians and social scientists are beginning to point out that many terrorist organizations engaging in transnational terrorism are heavily subsidized by several governments: some are, in fact, governmental branches. This in itself might lead to caution in the employment of weapons of mass destruction, since such employment could very likely precipitate countermeasures of such severity as to topple any government associated with the act.

Terrorist organizations not aligned with any particular government would still be constrained from the use of mass destruction weapons by factors considered earlier: risking the lives of their constituencies, excessive penalties, and loss of sympathy for the movement. It is difficult to discern any set of conditions short of sheer desperation which would systematically and logically lead terrorist groups to the conclusion that it was in their interest to employ a weapon of mass destruction.

With respect to the potential desperate use of such a weapon, several observations may be made. Ignoring scenarios leading to desperate measures, of which there are many, there are several requisite steps which must be taken before the desperate use of a mass destruction weapon may be made. The principal one is the advance preparation of contingency plans which encompass such a strategy. However, it does not seem likely that an organization would plan in advance for its own final hours. It is not in the nature of such organizations to plan for apocalyptic events.

There is, of course, the frequently cited scenario of terrorists holding a city or government hostage for purposes of extortion by threatening the use of a weapon of mass destruction. As must be apparent, however, there is still much fertile ground to be plowed by purely conventional means of hostage-taking for ransom. This is not to say, of course, that there is no upper bound.

Hostage-takers cannot, for example, demand more than can be paid; they cannot demand of a government more than the government's constituency is prepared to give. Nor can they demand the dissolution of a government, or even an effective major policy change, since such demands would tend to be unenforceable unless the terrorists could maintain a long-term enforcement capability, which seems rather unlikely.

Terrorists are undoubtedly aware of these considerations; the most capable terrorist organizations are politically astute. The more mass destruction weapon city- or government-hostage scenarios are examined, the more unlikely a proposition they seem to become.

What seems the most credible variation of this family of scenarios, however, is that in which a government might be held hostage for the release of political prisoners. In this case, there might be no money demand; the time for compliance could be relatively short; and once the demand was met, there would be no continuing requirement for the terrorists to maintain the threat. All of these factors work to the terrorists' advantage relative to all other city- or government-hostage scenarios which have had some currency in the past. This is not to say, however, that many other difficulties, both practical and political, do not stand in the way of perpetrating such a threat. Some of these have been discussed previously.

One of the questions that must be asked then, is what can transnational terrorists accomplish through the use of mass destruction terror that they could not accomplish with conventional military and guerrilla methods at less risk and cost, the almost certain increase in public abhorrence of such methods, and the potentially disastrous political reactions arising therefrom?

Insofar as indigenous terrorists are concerned, they would be under additional sets of constraints against the implementation of weapons of mass destruction. Since these groups operate almost entirely within their own countries, they must retain a reservoir of favorable public opinion in order to satisfy at least some of their objectives. Recent history shows several instances where conventional indigenous terrorist violence was curbed. Wohlstetter[46] points out that during the Cuban revolution, indiscriminate use of violence by the 26 of July Movement had to be curbed because of unfavorable public reaction. In Uruguay, the Tupamaros carried violence to a point that led to their virtual destruction. Violence perpetrated

by the Tupamaros reached such proportions that the Uruguayan government finally acceded to its army's request for special powers to destroy the movement—which was done, although at a considerable and continuing cost to civil liberties.[47]

Another factor contributing to the speculation surrounding the potential terrorist use of a mass destruction weapon which needs to be examined are terrorist technological resources, and the employment by terrorists of other than conventional, non-crew-served weaponry. For purposes of this discussion, manpower resources are not considered to be limiting.

With respect to weaponry, it may safely be stated that conventional munitions such as small arms, including automatic weapons, bulk explosives, and hand grenades are freely available to terrorists.[48] Such munitions are known to move relatively freely between sympathetic governments and terrorist groups, and between terrorist groups which, not infrequently, share munitions.[49] As is well-known, other weaponry is also available to terrorists. Shoulder fired missile launchers have, on rare occasions, been employed by terrorists, or terrorists have been apprehended with them in their possession.[50]

To the first point, it is apparent that some terrorist groups have always had available to them the conventional munitions of the day. Today, that means the latest in assault rifles, submachine guns, and other firearms, as well as sophisticated explosives in bulk, and man-portable military explosive devices such as hand grenades, demolition shaped charges, satchel charges, anti-personnel mines, and other devices. A somewhat surprising observation is, in spite of such availability, the last mentioned explosive devices are rarely used except in actions which may be supportive of civil wars or "wars of liberation." This observation bears on the following discussion.

With respect to the second point, we are frequently given to believe that less conventional weaponry is also available to terrorist groups more or less indiscriminately. That is to say, shoulder fired missile launchers, in part due to their widespread military use, high rate of manufacture, relative cheapness, and occasional use by terrorists, will come to be a primary weapon in the armamentaria of terrorist groups. This line of reasoning occasionally also extends to the future terrorist adoption of precision guided munitions such as the TOW, HOT, Blowpipe, and other optically or wire guided missiles. One may, however, look in vain for even modest use of portable missile launchers which have been around for decades.

To be sure, there have been instances of such use,[51] but the incidence of use does not point to an evolutionary step in increasing terrorist violence mediated by special weapons. To the contrary, the munitions types employed by terrorists have remained somewhat static over the decades, with the only evidence of an evolutionary trend being the adoption by terrorists of more recent small arms and similar munitions as these become available. The numbers of incidents where rocket launchers are employed are rare, no matter in what terrorist cause they may be used. Moreover, their rate of use remains relatively constant. One therefore observes that the level of terrorist violence has remained over the years relatively static; only the frequency of incidents has increased in the past decade.

One resource that may be limiting to almost all terrorist groups who would perhaps otherwise engage in incidents requiring some technical sophistication, is technological skill. Although terrorist groups are frequently composed of literate, educated, middle-class individuals, these people are most often educated in the social sciences and the humanities. In fact, if one searches for terrorist groups possessing technological and physical science skills, such will be found only in two or three relatively small groups in the mid-East.[52] This fact seems to influence the nature of terrorist tactics and target selection. It also seems to bear on the effectiveness of many terrorist incidents where the possession of even moderate technical abilities could have had marked effects on the outcome of an incident. It would also seem to bear on the capability of a terrorist group to embark on the construction and employment of a weapon of mass destruction. Such an undertaking, while in some instances requiring what the author would term only modest technological skills, are nevertheless levels of skill not apparent in terrorist organizations today or historically. It appears very much as though terrorist groups are simply incapable of mounting a credible mass destruction threat, based on technological resource requirements alone.

What then are we to make of the terrorist mass destruction threat? Aside from the technological problems, which at this time do not appear to be insignificant insofar as terrorists are concerned, there remain the political and constituent factors to consider in any strategy to employ a weapon of mass destruction. It simply strains the bounds of credulity to conclude that noninstitutional terrorist violence will evolve to a mass destruction capability. The indiscriminate effects of a mass destruction weapon would, it seems, in and of itself discourage its use for all but highly parochial and discrete targets. Even in such instances as these, the weapon must be chosen carefully and designed specifically for the job at hand. Thus, biologicals may be ruled out for use because of difficulties in controlling the spread of the effects of some agents. The employment of a nuclear device may require a weapon designed to have effects restricted to the target. Given that it appears at present there may not exist any terrorist group with the skills requisite for building a crude nuclear device of unpredictable yield, it would seem that it is simply beyond terrorist capabilities to design a weapon with a yield predictable within acceptable error limits.

It is not irrelevant to observe that the capacity for a single individual to cause an event of mass destruction has existed for at least two generations. In that time we have seen numerous unsubstantiated tales of terrorist threats or attempts to employ chemicals or biologicals against society at large, or against specific elements of society. In that time we have also seen such tales concerning the clandestine nuclear weapon.

In that time we have also seen, however, a plot to employ typhoid bacillus in metropolitan water supplies,[53] the manufacture of diisopropyl fluorophosphate by a criminal organization, which packaged the DFP in aerosol cans for use as assassination weapons,[54] the theft of mustard gas from a disposal site in Europe,[55] and unconfirmed reports of attempts to steal anthrax bacillus from Fort Detrick.[56]

Thus, although the possibility of a credible terrorist mass destruction threat seems remote in the extreme, we are nevertheless faced with something akin to a conundrum. On the one hand the possibility of a threat appears too remote to consider that a credible one will occur in the foreseeable future. On the other hand, the potential consequences of such a threat are greater than most natural disasters. The latter fact appears to be the driving force behind most analyses of potential terrorist mass destruction threats, suggestions for regulation of sensitive industries and materials, and for the development of contingency planning in the event of a credible threat.

While the author takes exception with a good deal of current and recent past analyses of potential terrorist mass destruction threat capability, it is felt that more effort than has heretofore been expended needs to be spent on: examining how sensitive non-nuclear materials are handled in commerce; what levels of accountability exist for their possession or use; where bureaucratic responsibilities lie for manufacturing, transport, possession and use of sensitive substances; the nature of responsiveness of the various bureaucratic strata to a credible mass destruction threat; how a threat is communicated from the receiver to an identifiable agency with clear cut responsibilities; how a threat assessment group is established to determine threat credibility; and on the development of sound crisis management policy[57] at various levels of government.

In summary, the potential terrorist mass destruction threat may be viewed as requiring various levels of technological skills depending on the nature of the threat. Requiring the greatest skills would be a credible threat involving a discriminate nuclear device. Considerably less skill would be required to precipitate a clandestine nuclear threat with a device of uncertain yield, and with some unknown probability of functioning in the nuclear mode. Fewer skills yet would be required to precipitate a credible mass destruction threat with either a chemical or biological agent. To date, such skills are felt to be beyond the capabilities of contemporary terrorist organizations.

These considerations are quite independent of political factors and constituent support following such use; indeed, the possibility of severe political consequences befalling such a constituency subsequent to such an event, forces one to the conclusion that the danger of non-institutional terrorist mass destruction threats are vanishingly remote.

This general conclusion needs to be qualified to the extent that the possibility such a threat could arise is also a function of geo-political, cultural, temporal, and economic factors. These cannot be considered in this paper. Therefore, while the general conclusion is felt to be a reasonable one, the same level of potential threat, while small, does not exist for all peoples and all nations.

But that subject is one of higher resolution than that treated here. It requires separate consideration.

NOTES

1. Richard Shultz, "Conceptualizing Political Terrorism: A Typology," *Journal of International Affairs,* (1978).

2. Mason Willrich and Theodore B. Taylor, *Nuclear Theft: Risks and Safeguards* (Cambridge, Mass: Ballinger Publishing Company, 1974); John McPhee, *The Curve of Binding Energy* (New York: Ballantine, 1974); Robert K. Mullen, *The International Clandestine Nuclear Threat,* Clandestine Tactics and Technology (Gaithersburg, MD: International Association of Chiefs of Police, 1975); *Idem, The Clandestine Use of Chemical or Biological Weapons,* Clandestine Tactics and Technology (Gaithersburg, MD: International Association of Chiefs of Police, in press).

3. Willrich and Taylor, op. cit.; McPhee, op. cit.

4. Willrich and Taylor, op. cit.

5. McPhee, op. cit.

6. John Larus, *Nuclear Weapons Safety and The Common Defense* (Columbus: Ohio State University Press, 1967).

7. U.S., Department of the Army, *Employment of Atomic Demolition Munitions (ADM) FM 5-26* (Washington, D.C.: Government Printing Office, 1971).

8. Jack Anderson, "Will Nuclear Weapons Fall Into The Hands of Terrorists?" *Parade,* Sept. 20, 1974; B. J. Berkowitz, et al., *Superviolence: The Civil Threat of Mass Destruction Weapons,* Adcon Corp. report A72-034-10, Sept. 29, 1972 (Santa Barbara, CA: The Adcon Corp., 1972).

9. E. Langer, "Chemical and Biological Warfare," *Science,* 155 (1967); U.S. House of Representatives, Committee on Government Operations, *Environmental Dangers of Open-Air Testing of Lethal Components* (Washington, D.C.: Government Printing Office, 1969).

10. F. Swarts, "Sur l'acide Fluoroacetique," *Bulletin of the Royal Academy, Belgium,* 31 (1896).

11. Frederick Lewis Maitland Pattison, *Toxic Aliphatic Fluorine Compounds* (New York: Elsevier, 1959).

12. Robert Thornton Morrison and Robert Neilson Boyd, *Organic Chemistry* (Boston: Allyn and Bacon, 1959).

13. Pattison, op. cit.

14. E. Chadwick, "Actions on Insects and Other Invertebrates," in *Cholinesterases and Anticholinesterase Agents,* Vol. 15, *Handbuch der Experimentallen Pharmakologie,* ed. by G. E. Koelle (Berlin: Springer-Verlag, 1963).

15. "Australian Police Nab Poison-Gas Producers," *Ottawa Citizen,* March 2, 1976.

16. K. P. DuBois, "Toxicological Evaluation of the Anticholinesterase Agents," in *Cholinesterases and Anticholinesterase Agents* Vol. 15, *Handbuch der Experimentallen Pharmakologie,* ed. by G. E. Koelle (Berlin: Springer-Verlag, 1963); D. Grob, "Anticholinesterase Intoxication in Man and Its Treatment," in *Cholinesterases and Anticholinesterase Agents,* Vol. 15, *Handbuch der Experimentallen Pharmakologie,* ed. by G. E. Koelle (Berlin: Springer-Verlag, 1963).

17. D. F. Heath, *Organophosphorous Poisons* (New York: MacMillan, 1961).

18. U.S., Department of Health, Education and Welfare, *Clinical Handbook on Economic Poisons* (Washington, D.C.: Government Printing Office, 1967).

19. Grob, op. cit.; Heath, op. cit.

20. Stockholm International Peace Research Institute, *The Rise of CB Weapons,* in Vol. 1, *The Problem of Chemical and Biological Warfare* (New York: Humanities Press, 1971).

21. Stockholm International Peace Research Institute, op. cit.

22. Stockholm International Peace Research Institute, op. cit.

23. Nicholas Wade, "Going Public with VX Formula—A Recipe for Trouble?" *Science,* 177 (1977).

24. Stockholm International Peace Research Institute, op. cit.

25. Stockholm International Peace Research Institute, op. cit.

26. P. J. R. Bryant, et al., "The Preparation and Physical Properties of Isopropyl Methylphosphono Fluoridate (Sarin)," *Journal of the Chemical Society (London)* (1960).

27. Bo Holmstedt, "Synthesis and Pharmacology of Dimethylamide-ethoxyphosphoryl Cyanide (Tabun)," *Acta Physiologica Scandinavica,* 25, Suppl. 50 (1952).

28. P. J. R. Bryant, op. cit.; Bo Holmstedt, op. cit.; R. Chosh and J. R. Newman, "A New Group of Organophosphorous Pesticides," cited in Berkowitz, et al., op. cit.; B. Holmstedt, "Structure-Activity Relationships of the Organophosphorous Anticholinesterase Agents," in *Cholinesterases and Anticholinesterase Agents,* Vol. 15, *Handbuch der Experimentallen Pharmakologie,* ed. by G. E. Koelle (Berlin: Springer-Verlag, 1963); A. H. Ford-Moore and B. J. Perry, "Diisopropyl Methylphosponate," *Organic Synthesis,* 31 (1951); *Idem,* "Triethyl Phosphite," *Organic Synthesis,* 31 (1951).

29. Stockholm International Peace Research Institute, *The Problem of Chemical and Biological Warfare* (New York: Humanities Press, 1971).

30. Hans Rieman, "Botulinum Types A, B and F," in *Infections and Intoxications,* ed. by Hans Rieman (New York: Academic Press, 1969).

31. G. Hobbs, Kathleen Williams, and A. T. Willis, "Basic Methods for the Isolation of Clostridia," in *Isolation of Anaerobes,* ed. by D. A. Shapta and R. G. Board (New York: Academic Press, 1971).

32. Richard Dean McCarthy, *The Ultimate Folly: War by Pestilence, Asphyxiation and Defoliation* (New York: Random House, 1969).

33. I. W. Dawes and J. Mandelstam, "Biochemistry and Sporulation of Bacillus subtilis 168: Continuous Culture Studies," in *Proceedings of the Fourth International Symposium on Continuous Cultivation of Microorganisms,* ed. by I. Malek, et al. (New York: Academic Press, 1969); J. Ricica, "Sporulation of Bacillus cereus in Multi-Stage Continuous Cultivation," in *Proceedings of the Fourth International Symposium on Continuous Cultivation of Microorganisms,* ed. by I. Malek, et al. (New York: Academic Press, 1969).

34. E. Langer, op. cit.

35. Mullen, *The International Clandestine Nuclear Threat,* op. cit.; Mullen, *The Clandestine Use of Chemical or Biological Weapons,* op. cit.

36. R. F. Phalen and O. G. Raabe, "Aerosol Particle Size as a Factor in Plutonium Toxicity," in *Proceedings*

of the Fifth Annual Conference on Environmental Toxicology, Aerospace Medical Research Laboratory Report ARML-IR-74-125 (Wright Patterson Air Force Base, Sept. 24, 1974).

37. U.S., Atomic Energy Commission, *Liquid Metal Fast Breeder Reactor Program Environmental Statement, WASH-1535,* Appendix II-g (Washington, D.C.: Government Printing Office).

38. Phalen and Raabe, op. cit.; National Academy of Sciences/National Research Council, *Health Effects of Alpha-Emitting Particles in the Respiratory Tract,* Report to the Environmental Protection Agency, EPA 520/4-76-013, 1976 (Washington, D.C.: Environmental Protection Agency, 1976); D. S. Myers, "The Biological Hazard and Measurement of Plutonium," in *Proceedings, Radiological Defense Officers Conference* (Lake Tahoe, CA: California Governor's Office of Emergency Services, 1974).

39. J. F. Park, W. J. Blair, and R. H. Busch, "Progress in Beagle Dog Studies and Transuranium Elements at Battelle-Northwest," *Health Physics,* 22 (1972).

40. Thomas M. Conrad, "Do-it-Yourself A-Bombs," *Commonweal,* July, 1969; Aland M. Adelson, "Please Don't Steal the Atomic Bomb," *Esquire,* May, 1969; Lowell Ponte, "Better Do As We Say: This is an Atom Bomb and We're not Fooling," *Penthouse,* Feb., 1972; *Idem,* "The Danger of Terrorists Getting Illicit A-Bombs," *Los Angeles Times,* April 25, 1976; Robert A. Jones, "Nuclear Terror Peril Likely to Increase," *Los Angeles Times,* April 25, 1976.

41. P. A. Karber, et al., "Analysis of the Terrorist Threat to the Commercial Nuclear Industry," *Draft Working Paper B, Summary of Findings,* Report to the U.S. Nuclear Regulatory Commission, The BDM Corp. Report BDM/W-75-176-TR (Vienna, VA: The BDM Corp., Sept., 1975); Miliaglo Mesarovic and Eduard Pestal, *Mankind at the Turning Point* (New York: E. P. Dutton, 1974); Brian Jenkins, *International Terrorism: A New Kind of Warfare,* Rand Corp. paper P-5261 (Santa Monica, CA: Rand Corp., June, 1974).

42. Brian Jenkins, "Will Terrorists go Nuclear?" (paper presented at California Seminar on Atomic Control and Foreign Policy, November, 1975); Robert A. Wohlstetter, "Terror on a Grand Scale," *Survival,* 18 (1976); Bernard L. Cohen, "The Potentialities of Terrorism,"

(Mimeographed); Eric D. Shaw, et al., "Analyzing Threats from Terrorism," CACI-Inc., April, 1976 (Mimeographed).

43. H. R. Simson, "Terror," *U.S. Naval Institute Proceedings,* 96 (1970).

44. N. Leites and C. Wolf, Jr., *Rebellion and Authority: An Analytic Essay on Insurgent Conflicts* (Chicago: Markham Publishing Company, 1970).

45. Wohlstetter, op. cit.

46. Wohlstetter, op. cit.

47. Brian Crozier, *Survey of Terrorism and Political Violence,* Annual of Power and Conflict, 1972–1973 (London: Institute for the Study of Conflict, 1973); Richard Clutterbuck, *Living with Terrorism* (London: Faber & Faber, 1975).

48. C. A. Russell, "Transnational Terrorism," *Air University Review,* 27 (1976); D. L. Milbank, *International and Transnational Terrorism: Diagnosis and Prognosis,* Central Intelligence Agency report PR 76 10031 (Washington, D.C.: Government Printing Office, 1976); S. Burnham, ed., *The Threat to Licensed Nuclear Facilities,* Report to the U.S. Nuclear Regulatory Commission, The Mitre Corporation report MTR-7022 (McLean, VA: The Mitre Corp., 1975).

49. Russell, op. cit.

50. Milbank, op. cit.; Burnham, op. cit.

51. Burnham, op. cit.; "2 Missiles Threaten Israeli Embassy," *Washington Post,* Dec. 13, 1977; "Philippine Terrorists Hit Oil Storage Tank," *Washington Post,* Dec. 13, 1977.

52. Charles A. Russell, Leon J. Baker, Jr., and Bowman H. Miller, "Out-Inventing the Terrorist," (paper presented at Terrorism Conference, Evian, France, June, 1977).

53. "Chicago Pair with Plot to Poison Midwest Water Supply," *Los Angeles Times,* Jan. 19, 1972.

54. *Ottawa Citizen,* op. cit.

55. "Terrorist Use of Gas Feared," *Washington Post,* April 13, 1975.

56. Berkowitz, et al., op. cit.

57. Robert H. Kupperman, "Crisis Management: Some Opportunities," *Science,* 187 (1975); *Idem,* "Treating the Symptoms of Terrorism: Some Principles of Good Hygiene," *Terrorism,* 1 (1977).

Chapter 6

THE LAWS OF WAR AS A POTENTIAL LEGAL REGIME FOR THE CONTROL OF TERRORIST ACTIVITIES*
Paul A. Tharp, Jr.

Over the past four years the sometimes bitter debate between the Western countries and the Third World states over the control of terrorism by international law has yielded few results; moreover, the positions of contending parties seem to have hardened. In an attempt to suggest a way out of this impasse, this essay will explore an alternative scheme for the regulation of international terrorism based on the laws of war. This idea is not new; the Third World states have used this approach in their positions on the issue in the various United Nations committees which have been working on draft resolutions and conventions.[1] Basically, the Third World sees "terrorists" as soldiers in wars of liberation against "alien, colonial and racist" national governments. The Third World states have been quick to assert the protective features of the laws of war *vis-à-vis* insurgent combatants but have virtually ignored the duties of such combatants to fight according to the rules of war.[2]

It is my intention to explore both the rights and duties imposed by the laws of war upon combatants and to try to draw analogies from the existing rules which might be applicable to the types of activities which we label as terrorism. I will also discuss some of the political "escape clauses" which have been suggested as ways to temper a code of law with political reality and humanitarian concerns.

The Traditional Approach to Terrorist Acts

Terrorism is not something new to the world scene. From ancient times to the present, political struggles have led to violent acts. Often the persons responsible for these acts have sought refuge in some friendly country or a holy place of sanctuary. With the advent of the modern nation-state in the 1600s, the problem of political fugitives (and other criminals as well) became a matter of criminal law to be applied by each state. Although some legal scholars argued that there was a customary duty to extradite fugitives, the prevailing practice from the 1600s to the present has been to base extradition upon treaties between the states involved.[3] This latter view, of course, is based upon the concept of sovereignty of each state. The laws of the state requesting extradition have no applicability in the sovereign territory of the requested state except to the extent that the requested state sovereign chooses to allow persons under his control to be subjected to the commands of another sovereign.

In addition to the concept of sovereignty, the French Revolution brought another issue into the problem of extradition. That was the impact of ideological differences between states. Prior to the French Revolution, the sovereigns of Europe held very similar political values. More often than not, the crowned heads of Europe protected each other by cooperating in the control of political activities which could be unsettling to the stability of their regimes. Exceptions, of course, were made for political fugitives who were political allies of the requested sovereign.

---

*This paper was originally prepared for the Nineteenth Annual Meeting of the International Studies Association, Washington, D.C., February 22–25, 1978.

With the French Revolution, ideological movements began to take shape within European countries which created the types of instabilities we know today.[4] Large scale political disturbances led to relatively large numbers of refugees who sought asylum in countries which were sympathetic to their cause. Thus, the concept of the "political crime" began to enter into the treaties of extradition wherein the requested state asserted the right to judge whether or not the fugitive was a common criminal or a person who was escaping political persecution.

By the early twentieth century, the laws of extradition had become quite complicated. A combination of the desire to preserve national sovereignty and ideological considerations caused governments to become incredibly legalistic in their examination of extradition requests. Let us examine a few of the major legalistic requirements.

1. Extradition treaties commonly were very explicit in listing the crimes which would be subject to extradition. Great Britain and the United States in particular insisted upon the so-called "list of offenses" approach. Continental practice was somewhat more flexible in that extradition was based in a few cases upon sovereign reciprocity or the notion that a particular crime violated norms which were shared by the societies of the requesting and requested states.[5]

2. States, particularly European countries, have often refused to extradite their own nationals. The rationale commonly used was that the person would not receive fair treatment in the foreign jurisdiction either because of nationalistic biases or judicial processes which were considered not to be of the same standards as the laws of the person's native state.[6] This did not mean that the defendant went unpunished. These same European states often held to the active nationality theory of jurisdiction which gives the native state the right to punish the misconduct of their citizens for acts done in a foreign state.[7] Also, in a few cases, the native state took judicial notice of the laws of the foreign state and applied them in a trial.

3. One of the most common reasons cited for non-extradition is the principle of double criminality.[8] Under this doctrine, the crime for which extradition is sought must be a crime in both the requesting and requested state.

4. Different standards of judicial due process and punishment can be troublesome.[9] For example, extradition has been refused in instances where the requesting state had the death penalty and the requested state did not (either in general or for that crime). Similarly, extradition has been refused on the grounds that the defendant would be subjected to double jeopardy or cruel and unusual punishment.

5. But for our purposes, the category which has been most difficult to operationalize has been the political offenses category which is seen as an exception to the treaties of extradition. In other words, even if the crime is one for which there can be extradition between the two countries, the injection of a political motive into the actions of the defendant may be used to exempt the defendant from the application of the treaty.[10]

The term "political offenses" is one of those slippery phrases in international law (like "innocent passage" in the law of the sea) which is frequently cited, but is basically undefinable. One class of political offenses is relatively easy to define. That is the "purely political" offense which very often does not involve violence.[11] It may simply be based on the defendant's political activities which his state regards as seditious, treasonable, or anti-regime. This type of crime is commonly treated as an offense for which extradition will be denied. When acts of violence become interwoven with the political act, the approaches of various states begin to differ widely. The traditional American/British approach is to examine whether or not the crime was "incidental" to the political act. This is usually interpreted to mean: was there a major political disturbance in the country in which the defendant participated which, unfortunately, led to acts of violence being committed against the civil authority and/or private persons?[12] The implications of the American/British approach are that the defendant should have been a part of an organized political disturbance and that the acts of violence were unfortunate by-products of that civil strife. The acts of a lone terrorist, or a covert group of terrorists, carried out against a society which is generally at peace internally might not qualify for denial of extradition under this legal test.

The traditional European approach has been more flexible and complex. The European courts have tried to determine if the political elements in the situation were preponderant over any intent to commit a common crime for personal gain. To determine the facts, these courts examine the purpose of the act and the means used to further that political objective.[13]

The purpose of this brief discussion of the traditional rules of extradition is to make the point that any attempt to control terrorism based on this approach (even in the form of multilateral treaties) is likely to be fruitless. It is the opinion of this writer that the body of law is too complex and the practices of states are too varying to be reconciled by international conventions. Moreover, the philosophical foundation for the rules of extradition is the concept of national sovereignty. Modern terrorism is clearly a transnational problem. The mobility of the terrorist may involve several national jurisdictions. The traditional rules of domestic criminality and extradition are simply not geared to situations where a multitude of national interests are violated.

The International Crimes Approach

The framework of international crimes could be considered as a possible scheme for the regulation of terrorist activities. Although the concept of international crimes dates back to the anti-slave trade and piracy treaties of the late 1700s and early 1800s, the concept has reached its present state of legal and philosophical articulation in this century.

The international crime concept is really three related concepts. There is a body of law which primarily deals with the acts of private individuals in the international system. Piracy, slavery and dealing in narcotics are examples. A second set of crimes refers to the acts of individuals acting in either some sort of governmental or private group capacity. War crimes and genocide are examples. Finally, there is an emerging concept, though one cannot yet say that these are crimes in the full juridical meaning of that word, which holds governments, as institutions, responsible for their treatment of human beings under their jurisdiction. The condemnation of apartheid in South Africa is a good example. For the remainder of this essay, I will refer to the first category above as private international crimes; the second can be referred to as "mixed" private/public crimes and the last category may be seen as governmental "crimes."

The international crime concept is based on the philosophical and pragmatic notion that certain rules must be upheld in the relations of nations if civilized intercourse is to be possible among peoples of the world. Sometimes the dominant factor is a concern for humanity as in the anti-slavery conventions of this century and the Nineteenth. Sometimes, the cause of a rule is purely pragmatic such as the anti-piracy treaties.

The single most important feature of the concept of international crimes is the establishment of a criminal justice procedure that transcends national jurisdiction and extradition problems. By custom or treaty (more commonly the latter) the nations of the world agree that certain persons must be apprehended and punished no matter where the act was done or where they are captured. The international community shares a collective responsibility to bring these people to justice. In essence each nation is waiving some of its sovereign rights *vis-à-vis* criminal law and national jurisdiction in the expectation that its neighbors will do the same in order to control a common problem.

In practical terms, an international crime—*even if politically motivated*—becomes an offense for which a country who has captured the defendant will extradite that person to another state which has a real interest in the person or the offense; or, if he is not extradited, then the state which has him in custody will prosecute him for the offense under its laws for similar types of crimes. This option to prosecute rather than extradite retains some aspects of sovereign discretion and political considerations which are found in the traditional law of extradition.

The norms which purport to hold governments responsible, in some collective sense, for their treatment of their own nationals or other persons under their control are not of the stature of criminal laws at this point in time. But, nonetheless, such conventions as the Racial Discrimination Convention, the Economic and Social Rights Covenent, and Civil and Political Rights Covenant are examples of what one might term as quasi-criminal norms of state behavior. However, these treaties might be regarded as growing evidence of general principles of law or international custom which could form the bases for collective sanctions under the Charter of the United Nations at some point in the future.[14]

At the present time, the United States' approach to the problem of terrorism has focused on the private international crimes approach. This involves three steps. First, the crime must be defined in rather specific legal terms, just as one would do in domestic legislation. Second, procedures for extradition or prosecution are established. Third, the political element is ruled out as a reason for failure to carry out the second step.

The United States' view is best seen in the complete draft of an international terrorism convention which the government submitted to the 1973 meeting of the Ad Hoc Committee on International Terrorism of the United Nations.[15] This draft proposes that any person who commits, attempts to commit or acts as an accomplice to the killing, seriously injuring or kidnapping of certain persons, has committed an international crime. The draft further defines the acts and persons to be protected. The offense must take effect outside of the territory of the alleged offenders' national state, or be committed outside of the territory of the state against which the act is directed, or be committed within the target state but against persons who are not nationals of that state. Acts committed by or against military personnel during military hostilities are not covered. Reference is also made in the document to the Geneva Conventions of 1949 and the specific applicability of those conventions to any alleged offender who might qualify for prisoner of war status. Article Three calls upon all parties to the convention to either extradite or prosecute the defendant, "without exception." Furthermore, there is no provision for asylum of any sort, nor reservations to the conventions, thus precluding any application of the various "political offenses" doctrines discussed above.

The Third World response to the American draft, then and now, has been to approach the problem as one of state criminality. The Third World states, including "moderates" such as Venezuela, see terrorism as a symptom of widespread government repression and denial of fundamental human rights. (Venezuela proposed including both private acts and governmental acts as grounds for an international crime;[16] the more radical states, such as Libya, Algeria, and Tanzania totally reject the private criminal law approach.) Basically the Third World states want the United Nations to elaborate additional norms in regard to state behavior and to begin enforcement of those norms through UN sanctions, including the possible use of coercive techniques. Furthermore, the basic Third World approach calls for some sort of international recognition of liberation movements (as in the case of the Palestinian Liberation Organization) and the applicability of the laws of war to liberation "soldiers" in the hands of a government, and to the conduct of "hostilities" in general between liberation movements and

states.[17]

Compromise Efforts

Over the past few years there have been some efforts to reach a compromise between the widely divergent views of the United States and its Western Allies and the prevailing opinion of much of the Third World. Both the Organization of American States and the United Nations conventions on the protection of diplomats begin with the basic private criminal law approach.[18] There are definitions of the classes of persons to be protected and the types of acts which will be regarded as offenses. There follows an obligation to extradite or prosecute. Also, such conventions contain provisions which obligate states to take steps to prevent their territory from being used as bases from which terrorist acts may be directed toward other states. However, these obligations are offset by provisions in both documents for the right of asylum. The OAS convention, reflecting the long-standing practice of asylum in Latin America, simply states: "None of the provisions of this Convention shall be interpreted so as to impair the right of asylum."[19] The UN document is more restrictive. The right of asylum is operative only between those states who have asylum provisions in treaties of extradition and those treaties are in force prior to the adoption by those states of the UN convention.[20]

If the right of asylum is narrowly interpreted to mean that states may refuse to extradite those persons who have been alleged to have committed "purely political" crimes such as one would commonly associate with non-violent forms of dissent and protest, then the asylum exception may be workable and does not conflict with the intent of the United States type of proposal which deals primarily with violent acts. On the other hand, the term "asylum" is a generic term in the law. It seems reasonable to assume that many states would include under that label any acts that they define as "political." Thus the exception becomes the rule.

The Council of Europe has produced a convention on terrorism which emerges as a genuine effort at compromise.[21] This 1976 document provides that the political offenses doctrine (including "purely" political offenses as well as various degrees of "mixed" political/criminal offenses) shall not apply to acts of violence associated with all forms of hijacking, attacks on diplomats, kidnapping, the taking of hostages or other offenses involving bombs, rockets, letter bombs, and other devices that endanger the general public. There follows, then, a standard reference to the duty to extradite or prosecute.

The harshness of the European convention is tempered by Articles Five and Thirteen. Article Five allows a party to the treaty to refuse to extradite the defendant if the requested state feels that the requesting state desires to prosecute the individual "on account" of his race, religion, nationality or political affiliation. Article Thirteen allows states to issue reservations to the provisions of the convention which pertain to the definitions of the crime and the general treatment of the political offense category. In other words, states can reserve the right to regard certain acts as political offenses as they have done under traditional international law and their treaties of extradition. However, the convention requests that a state which has such a reservation carefully examine the act involved to see if it is of such magnitude or callous disregard for innocent lives that it should be punished in some way. Specifically, the convention suggests the following test: (1) did the offense pose collective danger to many persons; (2) did the offense involve innocent third parties; and (3) was the offense particularly cruel or vicious? Therefore, the state with such a reservation must bear the burden of determining whether or not to waive its own reservation in such extreme cases and either extradite the individual or prosecute him under that state's own criminal laws.

The European approach to the political crime issue deserves careful scrutiny as a potential model for other agreements. It avoids such broad language as "asylum" and instead attempts to set forth a mixture of specific political and criminal criteria for states to use in borderline cases. Rather than judge the defendant's act from the standpoint of his political motivations, the convention specifically involves the interests of innocent parties and society in general. Although the "danger to society" criterion is implicit in some of the case law of traditional extradition, it is timely to make this an explicit criterion given the immense capacity for injury which the weapons and tactics of modern terrorism can employ.

The War Crimes Approach

There is another compromise to the problem of terrorism to be found in analogies to the laws of war. The difficulty with any of the approaches which use the private criminal law foundation (and that includes the European convention discussed above) is that they ignore the fact that many of these "terrorist" acts are acts of organized, prolonged "military" hostilities. Given the mobility of terrorists, these acts are very often ones of international war, in the sense that they involve allies of the terrorists and allies of the target state.

Applying criminal laws to the issue of terrorism presents other problems. Criminal laws have as their purpose the maintenance of legal norms which supposedly represent a community consensus as to what behavior the community will not tolerate. If political or other mitigating circumstances enter into the enforcement of these laws, then these cases are treated as exceptions to the general rules. It should be clear from the years of debate on terrorism and the history of extradition that no viable international community consensus exists in the area of political crimes. On the other hand, the laws of war evolved to serve a different set of needs in society. The purpose of the laws of war is to establish some minimal standards of conduct between two parties who have resorted to violence to settle their problems. Except for the attempts in the League of Nations and the UN to define aggression, the traditional rules of war did not attempt to fix blame on one of the parties for initiating or sustaining the conflict. The rules of war came into play after conflict had begun in order to mitigate the suffering of combatants and non-combatants.

Yet, there are ways in which the laws of war could be used to regulate terrorist activities,[22] including the following:

First: Certain categories of persons are to be protected. Combatants are under the obligation to avoid injury to innocent civilians. An enemy soldier, when he is rendered incapable of further combat, is to be treated as a POW. If he does not meet the tests for POW status (as most guerrilla/terrorists would not), then Article Three, common to all four Geneva Conventions of 1949, would come into play. This article provides for minimal humane treatment of combatants. Article Three also provides for minimal judicial due process should these combatants be placed on trial. (The problems of enforcement of these "minimal" provisions will be discussed shortly).

Second: Certain categories of targets are "off-limits" to the combatants. In traditional terms this refers to churches, schools, hospitals and other important public facilities. This concept could be expanded to cover aircraft, ships and other types of situations in which members of the public are highly vulnerable to mass destruction.

Third: Certain types of weapons are banned due to their inhumane characteristics or their indiscriminate application. Most terrorist weapons fit into this category.

Several problems arise, though, which need to be discussed.

First: If terrorists were obliged to obey the laws of war, then their military capabilities would be severely limited. The terrorist relies on the element of surprise and shock to overcome the powerful force of the government. The *quid pro quo* for the terrorist, of course, is the hope that he might be treated more humanely by governments if he is captured.

Second: The record of enforcement of the laws of war is generally dismal. Is there any reason to believe that either party to an insurgent war would abide by these rules?

Third: Granting combatant status to the insurgents may be construed as conferring some sort of international legal personality upon the group which, in turn, undermines the ability of the target government to treat this as a purely domestic matter. Thus governments may be as reluctant as insurgents to accept such a code of law.

These problems are formidable. The mechanisms of enforcement are potentially critical to the operation of an international convention on terrorism which is based on the laws of war. The problem which we are addressing has to do with the regulation of terrorists who have carried their activities into the international arena; third party states are involved either because the act took place under their jurisdiction or the defendant is in their custody. In other words, it may be possible to isolate the international aspect of the problem from the domestic aspect.[23] At least the laws of war approach may be usable in the former, while the latter problem may have to be dealt with in political forums, such as the United Nations.

How would a terrorism convention based on the laws of war be structured? The substantive sections would be straightforward restatements and adaptations of the laws of war to the environment of terrorism in which restraints would be placed on both the insurgents and the government *vis-à-vis* targets (persons and places) and

weapons and tactics. Furthermore, both sides would be obliged to extend minimal standards of treatment to captured combatants. Reference could be made to the Civil and Political Rights Covenant for articulation of those minimal standards to be applied in case of trials of prisoners, by the target state government or the liberation movement.[24]

In regard to the rights and duties of third party states, which have jurisdiction over an individual accused of violating these laws, the options would be extradition, prosecution, or asylum. However, the determination of each case would be based upon the defendant's conduct under the laws of war, rather than the political crimes tests employed in traditional extradition. The criteria found in Article Thirteen of the European convention, discussed above, seem to be appropriate as a supplementary set of general guidelines for the court to follow. Moreover, the "combatant" conduct of the state requesting extradition should be taken into account as mitigating factors. This would be similar to the rationale behind the protective provisions of Article Five of the European convention.

In other words, when we apply the laws of war to the acts of an individual, we judge his conduct as a soldier, not as a criminal. We accept as given that his actions are politically motivated to some degree; third parties then hold him accountable, or set him free, based on his performance as a combatant.

The laws of war framework might also be used to regulate the international reactions of the target state. Since July 1976, we have had three examples wherein governments staged anti-terrorist raids on the soil of another state. Two of these (Entebbe and Cyprus) involved casualties in one or both of the opposing national forces and an "invasion" of another sovereign's territory. Also present in the Cyprus case was the potential participation of another "irregular" force (the PLO commandos). Clearly, these types of situations bring terrorism into the realm of international armed conflict wherein the laws of war may be directly applicable.

Summary

Any scheme suggested to control the problem of terrorism is going to be difficult to sell to all members of the world community. No solution can be seen as inherently better than another proposal. However, it has been my contention that further reliance upon the traditional rules of extradition is unworkable, given the complexity of the laws, their nationalistic bases of jurisdiction and the undefined nature of what constitutes a "political crime." If we turn to the international crime approach, we begin to see ways of handling the situation on a multilateral basis which corresponds more closely to the nature of the problem. If we use the international private crime approach, then the new European convention seems to hold the greatest promise as a model document. It adequately defines the nature of the crime, yet leaves room for political and humanistic concerns without resorting to the loose language of asylum. Under the European approach the conduct of the defendant *vis-à-vis* the general public becomes a major factor, rather than the "nobility" of his political motives.

Finally, I have suggested that the most satisfactory approach of all may be the war crimes approach. Under this method, the political nature of the defendant's acts are accepted as being legitimate in some degree, but he is still to be held accountable for his actions in regard to those persons and institutions which the laws of war strive to protect. Moreover, the laws of war would apply equally to the conduct of governments, thus affording some international protection to the insurgent. Finally, the "mixed" private/public crimes approach to the laws of war offers a philosophical compromise between the legalistic private crimes approach taken by the United States and the ideological governmental "crimes" view of the Third World.

NOTES

1. The best collection of these views may be seen in United Nations, General Assembly, *Report of the Ad Hoc Committee on International Terrorism,* (XXVIII, A/9028—Supplement 28), 1973.

2. United Nations, General Assembly, *Basic Principles of the Legal Status of the Combatants Struggling Against Colonial and Alien Domination and Racist Regimes* (XXVIII, Resolution 3103), December 12, 1973.

3. M. Cherif Bassiouni, *International Extradition and World Public Order* (Dobbs Ferry, N.Y.: Oceana Press, 1974), see pages 6–9.

4. Ibid., p., 370 *et seq.*

5. M. Cherif Bassiouni, ed., *International Terrorism and Political Crimes* (Springfield, Ill.: Charles Thomas Co., 1975); S. Prakash Sinha, *Asylum and International Law* (The Hague: Nijhoff, 1971); I. A. Shearer, *Extradition in International Law* (Dobbs Ferry, N.Y.: Oceana Press, 1971).

6. Bassiouni, *International Extradition,* pp. 435–66.

7. Ibid., pp. 202–76.

8. Ibid., pp. 312–26.

9. Ibid., pp. 435–66.

10. Shearer, pp. 166–84; Sinha, pp. 170–203.

11. Bassiouni, *International Extradition,* pp. 379 *et seq.*

12. Ibid., pp. 388 *et seq.;* Shearer, p. 172 *et seq.*

13. Ibid., pp. 402 *et seq.*

14. The important thing to note about these various post-World War II human rights treaties is the expansion of categories to be regarded as international and the shrinking of the concept of exclusive domestic jurisdiction.

15. United Nations, General Assembly, *Ad Hoc* Committee on International Terrorism, pp. 28–33 (see footnote #1).

16. Ibid., p. 23.

17. United Nations, General Assembly, Resolution XXVIII. 3103 (see footnote #2).

18. Organization of American States, Convention to Prevent and Punish the Acts of Terrorism Taking the Form of Crimes Against Persons and Related Extortion That Are of International Significance, Washington, D.C., February 2, 1971 (found in U.N.-A/L 6/418 ANNEX 5), November 2, 1972; and United Nations, Convention on the Prevention and Punishment of Crimes Against Internationally Protected Persons (A/Res. 3166 XXVIII), December 14, 1973.

19. OAS Treaty, Article Six.

20. United Nations Treaty, Article Twelve.

21. Council of Europe, Convention on the Suppression of Terrorism, November 10, 1976, reported in 15 *International Legal Materials* 1272.

22. The four Geneva Conventions of August 12, 1949 are found in *TIAS 3362, 3363, 3364 and 3365.* Excellent, detailed interpretations of these conventions can be found in United States, Department of the Army, *The Law of Land Warfare* (FM 27-10), July 1956; and United States, Department of the Air Force, *International Law—The Conduct of Armed Conflict and Air Operations* (AFP 110-31) 19 November 1976.

23. Given the fact that many states would not be willing to apply these norms domestically but might be willing to apply them internationally, the use of optional clauses in regard to domestic application would be desired.

24. The Covenant on Civil and Political Rights, A/Res. 2200 (XXI) came into force (and the Optional Protocol as well), on January 3, 1976.

Chapter 7

TERRORISM, THE MEDIA AND THE POLICE*

Yonah Alexander

Terrorism, as an expedient tactical and strategic tool of politics in the struggle for power within and among nations, is not new in the history of man's inhumanity to man. From time immemorial opposition groups, functioning under varying degrees of stress, have intentionally utilized instruments of psychological and physical force—including intimidation, coercion, repression and, ultimately, destruction of lives and property—for the purpose of attaining real or imaginary ideological and political goals. That is, as agitational and disruptive civil violence, terrorism has been employed by sub-national groups either seeking to effect limited changes within the existing political structure, or desiring to abolish completely the established system, principally, but not exclusively, as part of a parochial or transnational revolutionary strategy.

Unlike older historical precedents, non-state terrorists, sanctified by their precipitators in the name of higher principles, have introduced into contemporary life a new breed of violence in terms of technology, victimization, threat and response. The brutalization and globalization of modern violence makes it amply clear that we have entered a unique "Age of Terrorism" with all its formidable problems and frightening ramifications. To be sure, it is generally recognized that extra-legal terrorism poses many threats to contemporary society and is likely to have a serious impact on the quality of life and on orderly civilized existence. Perhaps the most significant dangers are those relating to the safety, welfare and rights of ordinary people, the stability of the state system, the health and pace of eco-

nomic development and the expansion, or even the survival of democracy.[1]

But, in spite of various national and international efforts to deal with the dangers of terrorism, the level of non-state violence remains high. The reasons for these conditions are diverse but include at least ten factors: disagreement about who is a terrorist, lack of understanding of the causes of terrorism, the support of terrorism by some states, the existence of an international network of terrorism, the politization of religion, double standards of morality, loss of resolve by governments, weak punishment of terrorists, flouting of world law and the roles of the mass media.[2] While all these factors deserve serious and thorough study, this essay will focus on the interaction of terrorism and the media, specifically as related to current criminal justice processes.

Clearly, modern technology has provided terror groups with a critical communications instrument—the media—which willingly or unwillingly serve their specific or general propaganda and psychological warfare needs.[3] More specifically, the strategy of terrorism followed by sub-national groups does not prescribe instant victories over established regimes or states. On the contrary, the struggle for intended ends is seen as complicated and protracted. Terror groups, by their very nature, are too small and too weak to achieve an upper hand in an eyeball-to-eyeball confrontation on the battlefield. Since sheer violence can ac-

---

*Originally prepared for the 19th Annual Meeting of the International Studies Association, Washington, D.C.

complish little or nothing in terms of ultimate goals, an extension of the duration and impact of the violent deed is therefore mandatory in the terrorist strategy. As Walter Laqueur stated, "The media are the terrorist's best friend. The terrorist's act by itself is nothing; publicity is all."[4]

It is because of this realization that terrorist operations have been broadly symbolic rather than physically oriented. In relying on immediate and extensive coverage of television, radio and the press for the maximum amount of propagandizing and publicizing, terrorists can rapidly and effectively reach watching, listening and reading audiences at home and abroad and thereby hope to attain essentially one or two of the following communications purposes: First, to enhance the effectiveness of their violence by creating an emotional state of extreme fear in target groups, and, thereby, ultimately alter their behavior and dispositions, or bring about a general or particular change in the structure of government or society; and, second, to draw forcibly and instantaneously the attention of the "whole world" to themselves in the expectation that these audiences will be prepared to act or, in some cases, to refrain from acting in a manner that will promote the cause they presumably represent.

Terrorism, then, like advertising, increases the effectiveness of its messages by focusing on spectacular incidents and by keeping particular issues alive through repetition. Carlos Marighella, in his much publicized *Minimanual of the Urban Guerrilla*, gave a better insight into this strategy:

> The coordination of urban guerrilla action, including each armed action, is the principal way of making armed propaganda.
>
> These actions, carried out with specific and determined objectives, inevitably become propaganda material for the mass communications system.
>
> Bank assaults, ambushes, desertions and diverting of arms, the rescue of prisoners, executions, kidnappings, sabotage, terrorism, and the war of nerves, are all cases in point.
>
> Airplanes diverted in flight by revolutionary action, moving ships and trains assaulted and seized by guerrillas, can also be solely for propaganda effects.

He further elaborates:

> The war of nerves or psychological war is an aggressive technique, based on the direct or indirect use of mass means of communication and news transmitted orally in order to demoralize the government.

> In psychological warfare, the government is always at a disadvantage since it imposes censorship on the mass media and winds up in a defensive position by not allowing anything against it to filter through.
>
> At this point it becomes desperate, is involved in greater contradictions and loss of prestige, and loses time and energy in an exhausting effort at control which is subject to being broken at any moment.[5]

The utilization and manipulation of the media, as directed by Marighella and other proponents of political and ideological violence, have been followed by practically all terrorist movements. They have sought not only to spread fear among the primary target, but also to publicize their discontent as well as their ideologies with a view of making their violent deeds appear heroic.

One dramatic instance of media manipulation is the Patricia Hearst-SLA episode. Her kidnapping in February 1974 was used as a form of propaganda for the revolution of the SLA. The terrorists insisted that the media carry in full their messages—both tapes and printed material—lest the safety of the prisoner be jeopardized. For several years the media have continued to magnify the case out of proportion to its real significance, thus providing sensational mass entertainment and serving the publicity needs of the SLA and its successors as well. What is most disturbing about this case is the fact that the media have given a small group of criminal misfits a "Robin Hood" image and transformed it into an internationally known movement possessing power and posing an insurmountable problem to the authorities.

Also, overseas terrorist operations have not been carried out for the sake of immediate results or for the purpose of violence itself. Thus, in November 1975 the Montoneros in Buenos Aires kidnapped the industrial director of Germany's Mercedes-Benz there and released him after the company *inter alia* published advertisements in newspapers in Europe, Washington, D.C., and Mexico denouncing the "economic imperialism" of multinational corporations in developing countries.

In another episode, which occurred in February 1975, the Baader-Meinhoff terrorists kidnapped a West Berlin politician in order to secure the release of their imprisoned comrades and also "hi-jacked" a local television network. Describing this incident, one West German editor related that "for 72 hours, we lost control of the medium. We shifted shows to meet their timetable. [They demanded that] our cameras be in position to record each of the prisoners as they boarded a plane, and our news coverage had to include prepared statements of their direction."[6]

In light of the foregoing, it can be concluded that, in the final analysis, the communications purposes which at least revolutionary terror groups seek through the media are attention, recognition and legitimacy. As Weisband and Roguly succinctly observed,

> For the terrorist, the path to legitimacy is through one's reputation for resilience, for self-sacrifice and daring, for brutality, and, above all, for effective discipline over words and actions. The terrorist is his own torch and bomb; he ignites the flames of national passion and, if possible, of political sympathy, and he does it by violating universal human sensibilities. It is the credibility that violence produces, whenever it appalls that renders terrorism horrifying yet powerful and, if successful, self-legitimating.[7]

To what extent does the media's extensive coverage of terrorism have an impact on public attitudes? Although there is no definite answer to this question, according to nationwide public opinion polls conducted by Yankelovich, Shelly & White, Inc. with regard to American public attitudes towards the Palestine Liberation Organization (PLO),[8] there seems to be a close relationship, at least in terms of a greater awareness.[9]

The first poll in January 1975 was taken shortly after widespread media coverage of Yasir Arafat's triumphal appearance before the U.N. General Assembly in November 1974 with all the pomp and circumstance surrounding a head of state. The second poll was conducted a year later, toward the end of January 1976 after the U.N. Security Council had invited the PLO to participate in its debate on the Middle East. In the intervening period, the PLO had succeeded in gaining admission to other U.N. sponsored conferences and had opened offices in many countries in Europe and the third world. But the PLO was also becoming more and more embroiled in the Lebanese civil war which was increasingly in the news at the time.

As one might expect, the continuing attention given to the PLO by the mass media over the year was reflected in increased public awareness of the group's existence. In January 1975 only about one-half of the American public (52 percent) said that it had heard of the PLO. By January 1976 the

figure had gone up to 63 percent. Again, as might be expected, the higher the educational level of the respondents, the greater the likelihood that they are aware of the PLO, with 88 percent of college graduates answering in the affirmative.

Another major consequence resulting from extensive media coverage of terrorism is the exportation of violent techniques which, in turn, often triggers similar extreme actions by other individuals and groups. As Richard Clutterbuck asserted, "ideas travel . . . through the normal news media . . . people watching and listening to the reports get ideas about doing the same things themselves."[10] That is, the more publicity given to bomb scares, the more bomb scares there are likely to be, and reports about plane hijacking lead to more plane hijackings.

The excessive media coverage of the two attempts on President Ford's life in 1975 caused deep concern that this publicity might set off similar actions by other would-be assassins. As the then Vice President Rockefeller stated, "Let's stop talking about it. Let's stop putting it on the front pages and on television. Psychiatrists say every time there is any publicity, it is stimulating to the unstable." A similar view was expressed by the then Secretary of the Treasury, William E. Simon: "It's the responsibility of the press, certainly, to tell the American people indeed what is happening. . . . But when these people are glamorized on the front pages of our national magazines, I think that this has to be thought of as doing great harm."[11]

The Hanafi Muslim takeover of three buildings in Washington, D.C., in March 1977 also became a major media event with similar implications. "The media," Charles Seib of *The Washington Post* wrote, "were as much a part of it as the terrorists, the victims and the authorities. The news business did what it always does when it deals with violence, bloodshed and suspense: It covered it excessively."[12] Ambassador Andrew Young, expressing concern about the contagious effect of such coverage, stated that it is tantamount to "advertising to neurotic people" who are inspired to attempt "suicidal and ridiculous" acts.[13]

An estimate of such an impact on the mass audience was provided recently by an academic observer. He explained

> Typical reporting of a terrorist event here in the United States might reach an audience of, say, conservatively, 40 million people. What's the chance that it may come to the attention of some bor-

derline psychopath who may be stimulated to take part in some future episode? If we were to consider that just one-tenth of one per cent of the audience were borderline psychopaths, that would be 40,000 potential maniacs. If we took one one-thousandth of one per cent we've still got 400. If we took 1/100,000 of one per cent, we would still have the four that are necessary to carry out a typical terrorist episode.[14]

To be sure, because terrorism, however local, is by its very nature a world-wide theatrical attraction, it tends to encourage angry and frustrated groups beyond a particular country to undertake similar acts as a way out of their helplessness and alienation. For example, several weeks after Argentina's Montoneros removed the body of ex-President Pedro Aramburu to secure the return of Eva Peron's body from Spain, Burmese terrorists stole the body of U Thant for the purpose of using it in negotiations with the Burmese government.

Another major issue related to the problem of terrorism and the media is the particular interaction of both with police agencies. In every terrorist incident an inevitable critical relationship develops between the media responsible for reporting the episode and the law enforcement personnel handling the incident. Not infrequently, the media, especially broadcasters, hinder effective police responses to terrorist activities. The media can, for instance, have three detrimental effects in seige-management situations: interfere with on-going operations; exacerbate the pressure on the responsible authorities and contribute to impaired decision-making; and harass relatives of victims by pressing for interviews.

During the Hanafi episode the media unknowingly worked at cross purposes with official action. They furnished the terrorists with direct intelligence information by continuing on-site television coverage, thus adding to their feeling of power. The media also made direct telephone calls to the terrorists for interview purposes and thereby tied up communication between the police negotiators and the criminals.

Some details concerning this case were provided by Charles Fenyvesi, a reporter who had been a hostage at the B'nai B'rith building during the seige. He related

The most damaging case concerned the TV reporter who caught sight of a basket, lifted up by rope, to the fifth floor, where, the world later learned, some people evaded the round-up and barricaded themselves in a room. Their presence

apparently was not known to the gunmen, who held their prisoners on the eighth floor but patrolled the lower floors until late Wednesday afternoon. The gunmen were probably informed of the TV reporter's scoop by their fellow Hanafis who monitored the news media outside the captured buildings. Fortunately the gunmen did not break through the door.

Another case of a reporter endangering lives occurred when Khaalis was asked, during a live telephone interview with a leading local radio station, 'Have you set a deadline?' The police and all the other experts have thought that the absence of a deadline was one encouraging sign. Fortunately, Khaalis was too engrossed in his rhetoric to pay any attention to the question.

A third example: One prominent Washington newscaster called Khaalis a Black Muslim. Khaalis, whose family was murdered by Black Muslims, flew into a rage and stormed into the room where we hostages were held. He declared that he would kill one of us in retaliation for the newsman's words. The police, meanwhile, advised the newscaster to promptly issue an apology, and Khaalis was eventually mollified.[15]

Robert L. Rabe, Assistant Chief of Police, Metropolitan Police Department, who was personally involved in handling the incident, complained about another instance of media irresponsibility during the Hanafi siege: "... a local reporter took it upon himself to report live over the radio and television what appeared to him to be boxes of ammunition being taken into the B'nai B'rith building in preparation for an all-out police assault, when, in fact, what was being taken were boxes of food for the hostages. Just imagine what the repercussions could have been if the terrorists had been monitoring their radios and televisions at that precise moment."[16]

It is noteworthy that, after the Hanafi hostages were freed, they were warned by the police not to give interviews to the media lest the prosecutor's task in dealing with the case become more difficult and complicated. According to complaints by the hostages, some members of the media were insistent on obtaining interviews. In one particular case, a network representative justified his request for an interview by asserting that "the public has the right to know." The harassed hostage declined to grant the interview, replying "Is it in the Constitution that the public has the right to invade my privacy, to insist on exposing people already humiliated, to wallow in their pain and misery?"[17]

Finally, it is also evident that the media have

jeopardized the authorities' management of terrorist incidents abroad. In the October 1977 hijacking of the Lufthansa jet, for instance, the media directly contributed to the death of a hostage because they did not realize that certain information, especially in regard to tactical operations, had to remain outside public knowledge. In this case, the terrorists on board the jet heard over the public radio broadcasts to which they had access that the German Captain was passing valuable intelligence information to the authorities on the ground through his normal radio transmissions. Subsequently, the terrorists executed the Captain.

To be sure, the roles of the media are not always detrimental. There are situations where the media, by publicizing an incident, have, in the words of Special Agent of the FBI, Conrad Hassel, "relaxed the pressure of the terrorist finger."[18] Also, Harold Coffman, Professor of Law and Psychiatry at Georgetown University, has stated ". . . that coverage of such events is helpful. It allows these people to have some method of ventilating their anger and frustration, in making known their grievances. The more coverage given, the more they are likely to see themselves part of, rather than outside, the system."[19]

One such example is the Croatian TWA case of September 1976. Here, the hijackers insisted that specific demands be accomplished as the price for terminating the hijacking, including, *inter alia,* that two propaganda tracts be published on the front page of a number of newspapers. *The New York Times, The Washington Post* and *The Chicago Tribune,* to mention a few, compiled and thereby contributed to a satisfactory management of the incident.

The media also played a helpful role in establishing a vital link between authorities and the public-at-large in connection with the May–June 1977 South Moluccan incident in Holland. During that episode daily news releases containing bits of information on details not crucial to developing strategy and tactics satisfied the public appetite for information, as well as conveyed an image of official responsibility and effective crisis management.

In light of these ramifications, the question is what role should the media in democratic systems have in combating terrorism? Two major problems must be considered in this connection. First are the facts that, to terrorists, an extensive coverage by the media is the major reward and

that "establishment" communications channels willingly or unwillingly become tools in the terrorist strategy, and that advertising terrorism increases the effectiveness of its message through repetition and imitation. The second concerns the vital importances of protecting "people's right to know" and of a free press in open societies. A closely critical issue is the relationship between the media and law enforcement agencies. Although each has a duty to perform and a right to perform that duty, the legitimate roles of both entities are seemingly diametrically opposed.

In sum, how can the media in a democratic society devise new methods of fair and credible reporting of terrorist activities without jeopardizing their responsibilities to the public and without adversely affecting the current criminal justice processes.

It is obvious that there are no easy answers to these vital concerns but most difficult choices. Indeed, the various issues have been highly controversial. For example, in April 1977 a Gallup poll found that Americans were divided about whether the media should give complete, detailed coverage of terrorism.[20] More definitive in their responses are the administrators of justice personnel. Thus, among the results of a survey of the police chiefs in some thirty American cities, the following views are emphasized:

1) 93 percent of the police chiefs believed live TV coverage of terrorist acts encourage terrorism.

2) None of the big-city police chiefs surveyed believed that coverage of terrorist acts should be televised live. Sixty percent thought such TV coverage should be delayed or video taped, and 27 percent believed terrorist acts should not be covered by television.

3) Forty-six percent of police chiefs consider live television coverage of terrorist acts "a great threat" to hostage safety and 33 percent considered it "a moderate threat." Only 7 percent considered it a minimal threat.

4) More than half of the police chiefs had generally unfavorable judgments of on-the-scene television reporters covering terrorists. Twenty percent of the police chiefs believed television reporters covering terrorist acts were "poor" and 33 percent believed they were "average." Only 20 percent believed that TV journalists covering terrorists were good.

5) Sixty-seven percent of the police chiefs said TV journalists should only communicate with ter-

rorists with official consent. Another 33 percent believed that under no circumstances should TV journalists communicate with terrorists while they are engaged in criminal activity.[21]

Although this survey is limited in scope, it is reasonable to assume that, in general, law enforcement agencies, which now lack both the legal authority and the practical ability to control coverage of terrorist activities, look upon the media "as a powerful force, sometimes more influential than government itself,"[22] which should somehow be restrained. This apparent attitude was underscored by Ambassador Andrew Young's assertion that "the First Amendment has got to be clarified by the Supreme Court in light of the power of the mass media," and that they should censor themselves.[23]

To be sure, some newsmen seem to realize that the media have much too much influence in domestic and international affairs.[24] A few are even prepared not to cover terrorism at all. One television news director in Cleveland explained, "We feel that the coverage we give such incidents is partly to blame, for we are glorifying lawbreakers, we are making heroes out of nonheroes. In effect we are losing control over our news departments. We are being used."[25]

While most journalists recognize the perils involved in covering terrorist incidents, the media in general reject as unthinkable any suggestion that would curtail their reporting. The National News Council, for example, warned that, "the dangers of suppression should be self evident: doubts over what the media have withheld and the motives for such a blackout; questions about other types of news which might also have been withheld ostensibly in the public interest; and the greater possible risks involved in wild and reckless rumors and exaggerated, provocative word-of-mouth reports."[26]

To some journalists even the suggestion that guidelines be adopted as one way to prevent excesses in terrorist-incident-coverage implies censorship and, ultimately, suppression. This sentiment was expressed by A. M. Rosenthal, executive editor of *The New York Times:* "The last thing in the world I want is guidelines. I don't want guidelines from the government and I don't want any from professional organizations or anyone else. The strength of the press is its diversity. As soon as you start imposing guidelines, they become peer-group pressures and then quasi-legal restrictions."[27]

In light of these and similar concerns, it is highly unlikely that governments in Western democracies, believing that free and dynamic media are vital to the success of their systems, will institute any form of official management of news. It has been reported, for instance, that President Carter "has no desire to seek legislation or to otherwise impose a solution and hopes those who make news decisions will themselves determine definable boundaries of legitimate coverage."[28]

A rare example where a democratic government has requested a news ban occurred in connection with the Schleyer kidnapping and the Lufthansa hijacking in October 1977. In this case the threat of terrorism was so grave that the West German government, for the first time ever, appealed to the media to impose a strict silence on themselves. This request was almost universally accepted. Subsequently, the government published, as originally promised, a detailed account of the events and decisions related to these specific terrorists incidents.[29]

In spite of this unique experience, the complex question of the role of the media as influencing terrorist results and societal initiative behavior remains largely unresolved. Admittedly, the interaction between the media and domestic violence has been a subject of serious discussion and substantial research since 1968. The various studies produced have, indeed, provided insightful data and a basis for further investigation in this important field.[30] Yet, the problem of how the media should function under terrorist-crisis conditions, particularly as they affect incident-management situations, has not, thus far at least, been suitably explored and systematically studied. Only isolated initiatives have been undertaken in this connection. Several conferences and limited research activities have dealt with some aspects of the problem.

In June 1976 the City University of New York (The Ralph Bunche Institute on the United Nations) and the State University of New York (The Institute for Studies in International Terrorism) co-sponsored a Conference on "Terrorism" in New York City supported with a grant from the Rockefeller Foundation. The Conference brought together scholars and authorities from universities, institutes, the United Nations, the media, and the legal and diplomatic professions. Important personages participating included Senator Jacob Javits, former Attorney General Ramsey Clark, Correspondent Pauline Frederick, and many others of comparable status. One spin-off result from this meeting was the publication of a book, *Terrorism: Interdisciplinary Perspectives*, which includes a chapter on the role of the media.[31]

Both universities, in cooperation with *The Courier-Journal, The Louisville Times,* and The American Jewish Committee (Institute on Human Relations) also organized a Conference on "Terrorism and the Media," in November 1977. Among those participating in the program were Robert H. Kupperman (U.S. Arms Control and Disarmament Agency), Peter Schlem (Assistant U.S. Attorney, Brooklyn), Captain Thomas M. Ashwood (Airline Pilots' Association, International), Dr. Frank M. Ochberg (National Institute of Mental Health), Professor Arthur M. Schlesinger, CBS correspondent Richard C. Hottelet, Robert Kleiman of *The New York Times,* Norman Isaacs of The National News Council, and many others. The meeting dealt with the tension between two major concerns—the media as a tool in the terrorist strategy and the importance of protecting "people's right to know." The proceedings of this gathering will be published in the Summer of 1978.

Another meeting on "The Media and Terrorism" was organized in Spring 1977 by James Hoge, editor-in-chief of *The Chicago Sun-Times* and *Chicago Daily News,* and Marshall Field, publisher of Field Enterprises, Inc. The day-long seminar included local and national experts from the fields of law enforcement, criminal law, and the media. A report was subsequently published and the sponsors also developed standards for *The Sun-Times* and *Daily News* coverage of terrorist acts, especially those involving hostages.[32]

Similarly, The Oklahoma Publishing Company (*The Daily Oklahoman-Oklahoma City Times*) co-sponsored a Seminar on "Terrorism: Police and Press Problems." Held in April 1977, this workshop aimed at dealing with the problems and causes of terrorism and at stimulating an exchange of needs and concerns between the press and the official sector. The overall purpose of this meeting was, in the words of Charles C. Bennett, Executive Editor of *The Oklahoman* and *Times,* "to create the highest level of preparedness in Oklahoma City in the event of future terrorist activity."[33]

In May of the same year, the Maryland Chapter Society of Professional Journalists sponsored a panel session on "Police Relations with Press" at the meeting of the Maryland-Delaware-D.C. Press Association, held in Ocean City, Maryland.[34] Another meeting on "Terrorists and Hostage Coverage," held in Washington, D.C., in Fall 1977, was organized by the Radio-Television News Directors' Association (RTNDA).[35]

These gatherings, as well as similar initiatives, have generated useful suggestions for responsible reporting of terrorist incidents. Moreover, some news organizations even adopted specific policies with a view of better managing such situations. In addition to *The Chicago Sun-Times* and *Chicago Daily News* already mentioned, *The Courier-Journal* and *The Louisville Times,* United Press International and CBS News have also unilaterally determined internal guidelines for coverage.[36] Other media entities such as *The Washington Post* and WMAL-TV of Washington, D.C., have established temporary rules to handle specific incidents as, for instance, the Hanafi episode.[37]

Finally, the research conducted by scholars on this subject is rather fragmentary, consisting of portions of reports,[38] occasional articles[39] or several chapters in books.[40] Perhaps the most comprehensive study is *Disorders and Terrorism,* published by the National Advisory Committee on Criminal Justice Standards and Goals.[41] While the task force examines some aspects of news coverage during commission of acts of terrorism, contemporaneous coverage and follow-up reporting,[42] it fails to assess fully the role of the media as they affect the management of terrorist activities by the authorities.

While the foregoing activities over the past several years are, indeed, commendable for contributing preliminary relevant material in this important area of public concern, there exists no multidisciplinary data-base of past efforts, no serious analysis of success and failure of handling specific terrorist incidents from the perspectives of the media and law enforcement officials themselves, and no acceptable and tested models of media and policy management of terrorist situations. In view of this condition, there is an immediate need to undertake a rigorous study on the interaction of terrorism, the media and police, and thereby fill the gap in scholarship pertinent to current criminal justice processes. A new urgency is given to this need by the warning of Walter Scheel, President of West Germany: "unless this flame [of terrorism] is stamped out in time, it will spread like a brush fire all over the world."[43] Indeed, this message forces us to ponder the future with grave concern and to determine appropriate courses of action.

In conclusion, any research undertaken in connection with terrorism and the media should take into account the following major observations and considerations: First, terrorism is essentially violence for effect and is directed not only at the instant victims of it and their family members but, by extension, also at a wider audience. Second, terrorism is a theater, at least in its embryonic stages, and, consequently, terrorists are making a conscious and deliberate effort to manipulate the media for their intended ends. Third, as the media are an industry based on competition and profit, it is inevitable that they become an integral part of any terrorist act, providing star actors, script writers and directors. Fourth, by providing extensive coverage of incidents the media give the impression that they sympathize with the terrorist cause, thereby creating a climate congenial to further violence. Fifth, the media often hinder the work of law enforcement agencies, thus jeopardizing successful outcomes of incidents. Sixth, the media have occasionally been helpful to the authorities in managing incidents without abandoning their responsibilities to the public's right to know. Seventh, the media should objectively, accurately and credibly report about ter-

rorist acts lest the public panic and lose trust and confidence in both the press and government. Eighth, any attempts to impose media blackouts are likely to force terrorists to escalate the levels of violence in order to attract more attention. Ninth, since a major goal of terrorism is to undermine authority and cause anarchy, an unjustifiable limitation or even destruction of free media will ultimately result in the victory of terrorism. Tenth, the media, without surrendering their prerogatives, should help criminal justice processes in dealing with terrorism, and, conversely, the administration of justice officials should turn to the media for professional assistance in handling incidents and in limiting their derivitive societal repercussions. Eleventh, given the nature and complexity of modern terrorism, the determination of a proper role for the media should not be left to their judgment alone, nor is it desirable that law enforcement agencies should unilaterally develop policies on this matter. And, twelfth, the threat of contemporary terrorism requires the openness, understanding and cooperation of both the media and criminal justice authorities, as well as many other segments of society, so that we can deal with this important area of public concern more hopefully and realistically.

NOTES

1. For details see Yonah Alexander, ed. *International Terrorism,* (New York: Praeger Publishers, 1976); Yonah Alexander and Seymour M. Finger, *Terrorism: Interdisciplinary Perspectives* (New York and London: John Jay Press and McGraw Hill, 1977); and Yonah Alexander and Herbert M. Levine, "Prepare for the Next Entebbe," *Chitty's Law Journal,* Vol. 25, No. 7 (September 1977); and Yonah Alexander, Editor-in-Chief, *Terrorism: International Journal,* Vol. 1, Nos. 1 (November 1977) and 2 (February 1978).

2. The mass media in a broad context includes newspapers, magazines, books, radio, television and films. For the purposes of our discussion we are concerned with the news media. Hereafter we shall use the term "media."

3. For a case study of the interaction between communications instruments and politics see, for example, Yonah Alexander, *The Role of Communications in The Middle East Conflict: Ideological and Religious Perspectives* (New York: Praeger Publishers, 1973).

4. "The Futility of Terrorism," *Harpers,* Vol. 252, No. 1510 (March 1976), p. 104.

5. Carlos Marighella, *Minimanual of the Urban Guerrilla,* Havana Tricontinental, n.d., p. 103. For a similar discussion see: Jerry Rubin, *Do It!* (New York: Simon and Schuster, 1970).

6. Quoted in Neil Hickey, "Terrorism and Television," *TV Guide,* July 31, 1976, p. 4.

7. Edward Weisband and Damir Roguly, "Palestinian Terrorism: Violence, Verbal Strategy, and Legitimacy," in Alexander, *International Terrorism,* supra note 1, pp. 278–279.

8. One may regard the PLO as a terrorist organization or as guerrillas according to the measures of one's identification with the cause involved in this particular case. The U.S. Government, thus far at least, considers the PLO a terrorist movement.

9. Remarks by George E. Gruen delivered before the Conference on "International Terrorism" organized by the City University of New York and the State University of New York, June 10, 1976.

10. "Terrorism is Likely to Increase," *London Times,* April 10, 1975.

11. Quoted in *The New York Times,* October 8, 1975.

12. Charles B. Seib, "The Hanafi Episode: A Media Event," *The Washington Post,* March 18, 1977, p. A27.

13. *The New York Times,* March 15, 1977.

14. Michael T. McEwen's statement before a Seminar on "Terrorism: Police and Press Problems" sponsored by the Oklahoma Publishing Company and the University of Oklahoma, April 14, 1977. Unpublished Proceedings, p. 32.

15. Quoted in "The Media and Terrorism," Proceedings of a Seminar sponsored by *The Chicago Sun-Times* and *The Chicago Daily News* (Spring 1977), pp. 28–29.

16. Remarks by Robert L. Rabe presented at the Conference on "Terrorism and the Media" sponsored by the Ralph Bunche Institute on the U.N. (The City University of New York) and the Institute for Studies in International Terrorism (State University of New York) and held at the Graduate Center of The City University, November 17, 1977.

17. Quoted by Charles Fenyvesi in remarks presented at the Conference on "Terrorism and the Media." See supra, note 16.

18. Stated by Conrad Hassel at a Seminar on "Terrorism and Business" sponsored by the Center for Strategic and International Studies (Georgetown University) and the Institute for Studies in International Terrorism (State University of New York), held in Washington, D.C., December 14, 1977.

19. Quoted at the Seminar on "Terrorism: Police and Press Problems," see supra, note 14, p. 65.

20. Reported in *Editor and Publisher,* August 27, 1977, p. 12.

21. *Ibid.*

22. Robert L. Rabe statement at the Conference on "Terrorism and the Media." See supra note 16.

23. *The New York Times,* March 15, 1977.

24. See, for example, Barry Sussman, "Media Leaders Want Less Influence," *The Washington Post,* September 29, 1976, p. A-1.

25. Philip Revzin, "A Reporter Looks at Media Role in Terror Threats," *The Wall Street Journal,* March 14, 1977, p. 16.

26. The National News Council, "Paper on Terrorism," March 22, 1977, unpublished document.

27. David Shaw, "Editors Face Terrorist Demand Dilemma," *The Los Angeles Times,* September 15, 1976, p. 14.

28. *The New York Times,* March 15, 1977.

29. *The German Tribune,* November 13, 1977.

30. The list of research in this area includes, for instance, U.S. National Advisory Commission on Civil Disorders, *Report* (Washington, D.C.: U.S. Government Printing Office, 1968); thirteen volumes of reports from the U.S. National Commission on the Causes and Prevention of Violence, especially D. L. Lange, R. K. Baker, and S. J. Ball, *Mass Media and Violence: A Staff Report to the National Commission on the Causes and Prevention of Violence,* Vol. 9 (Washington, D.C.: U.S. Government Printing Office, 1969); U.S. Surgeon General's Scientific Advisory Committee on Television and Social Behavior, *Television and Social Behavior: Technical Reports to the Committee,* 5 vols. (Washington, D.C.: U.S. Government Printing Office, 1972); Otto Larsen, ed., *Violence and the Mass Media* (New York: Harper and Row, 1968); and Charles U. Daley, ed., *The Media and the Cities* (Chicago: University of Chicago Press, 1968).

31. Yonah Alexander and Seymour M. Finger, *Terrorism: Interdisciplinary Perspectives, op. cit.,* pp. 141–206.

32. *The Media and Terrorism.* A Seminar sponsored by *The Chicago Sun-Times* and *Chicago Daily News* (Chicago: Field Enterprises, 1977).

33. Charles L. Bennett's letter of invitation to invited participants, March 18, 1977.

34. *Editor & Publisher,* September 17, 1977.

35. *Broadcasting,* September 26, 1977.

36. For a text of these guidelines see The National News Council, supra, note 26.

37. For other policy positions of news organizations see, for example, Ina Meyers, "Terrorism in the News,"

The Daily Times (Mamaroneck, N.Y.), April 2, 1977.

38.   See, for example, Robert J. Jackson, et al., *Collective Conflict, Violence, and the Media in Canada* (Ottawa, Ont.: Carleton University, n.d.).

39.   See, for instance, Yonah Alexander, "Communications Aspects of International Terrorism," *International Problems,* Vol. 16, Nos. 1–2 (Spring 1977), pp. 55–60, and H. H. A. Cooper, "Terrorism and the Media," *Chitty's Law Journal,* Vol. 24, No. 7 (1976), pp. 226–232.

40.   See, for example, Alexander and Finger, supra, note 31, and Cherit Bassiouni, *Terrorism and Political Crimes* (Springfield, Ill.: Charles C. Thomas, 1975), pp. 43–46.

41.   *Disorders and Terrorism,* Report of the Task Force on Disorders and Terrorism (Washington, D.C.: National Advisory Committee on Criminal Justice Standards and Goals, 1976).

42.   *Ibid.,* pp. 366, 387–388, 401–402.

43.   Quoted in *The New York Times,* October 25, 1977.

Do you really know what your children were doing last night?

Maybe you think that your teenage sons or daughters couldn't find themselves in jail for serious crimes.

In Northern Ireland last year a great many parents thought just like you — and they were wrong!

A short time ago there were over 300 teenagers in Ulster jails convicted of crimes ranging through murder, explosives offences, firearms offences and armed robbery.

Many more could be there - but they blew themselves up.

If you've no time for your children —SOMEONE ELSE HAS!

ISSUED BY THE NORTHERN IRELAND OFFICE

Chapter 8
INTERNATIONAL TERRORISM:
Trends and Potentialities
Brian M. Jenkins

Political fanatics have demonstrated repeatedly in the last few years that by employing terrorist tactics they can achieve disproportionate effects in the world. They have attracted worldwide attention to themselves and their causes. They have caused worldwide alarm. They have compelled governments to negotiate with them and often to grant them concessions. Very much the phenomenon of the 1970s, will terrorism persist? Forecasts as to whether or not terrorism will persist depend largely on one's analysis of the origin and nature of modern international terrorism.

Some perceive today's terrorism as the outgrowth of unique political circumstances prevailing in the late 1960s: the Israeli defeat of the Arabs in 1967, which caused Palestinians to abandon their dependence on Arab military power and turn to terrorism; increasing emphasis on urban guerrilla warfare in Latin America, and with it, the resort to terrorist tactics; and the anti-Vietnam war and anti-government demonstrations in Western Europe, Japan, and the United States which ultimately spawned terrorist groups such as the Baader-Meinhof Gang and the Japanese Red Army. According to this view, terrorism will decline as political circumstances change, as original conflicts are resolved, as governments effectively combat terrorism.

If, on the other hand, the current wave of terrorism is seen as the result, not only of unique political circumstances, but also of recent technological developments—international travel giving terrorists worldwide mobility; improved mass communications providing them with almost instantaneous access to a worldwide audience; the increasing availability of weapons and explosives; and new vulnerabilities in a society increasingly dependent on fragile technology—or if terrorism is seen as a new set of tactics whose use inspires other groups—then terrorism is likely to continue.

My own view is that the use of terrorist tactics will persist as a mode of political expression, of gaining international attention, and of achieving limited political goals. Although no terrorists have achieved their stated long-range goals, and in that sense have failed, their use of terrorist tactics has won them publicity and occasional concessions. These tactical successes probably will suffice to preclude the abandonment of terrorist tactics.

Bombing probably will remain the most common terrorist tactic. Explosives can be easily purchased, stolen, or manufactured from commercially-available materials. Knowledge of at least primitive explosives is widespread. Bombings require little organization; it can easily be a one-man operation.

Seizing hostages whether by kidnapping individuals, hijacking airliners, or storming buildings also will continue to be a popular terrorist tactic owning to its demonstrated effectiveness. In dealing with hostage incidents, governments appear to be increasingly willing to respond with force. The last two years have seen the increasing use of special police and military commando units to storm airliners and buildings seized by terrorists. Fourteen of the 25 interactional hostage situations that have occurred since the beginning of 1976 were ended by force. This trend seems likely to continue.

Terrorists will remain mobile, able to strike targets anywhere in the world. They appear to be getting more sophisticated and strengthening their links with each other. "Freelance" terrorists may emerge. It is also possible that some nations in the future may employ terrorist groups as a mode of surrogate warfare. Although we may foresee an era of formal peace between nations, we may at the same time be entering an era of increased political violence at lower levels.

Whether terrorism itself will increase largely depends on how one counts. The decade from the beginning of 1968 to the end of 1977 saw an increase in international terrorism if we simply go by the number of incidents. The increase is not steady. It traces a jagged line of peaks and valleys, but the trend is upward (See Figure 1).

These are incidents of international terrorism only, that is, incidents in which terrorists cross national frontiers to carry out their attacks, select victims or targets because of their connections to a foreign state (diplomats, executives of foreign corporations, embassies), attack airliners on international flights, or force airliners to fly to another country. It excludes the considerable amount of terrorist violence carried out by terrorists operating within their own country against their own nationals, and in many countries by governments against their own citizens. For example, Irish terrorists blowing up other Irishmen in Belfast would not be counted, nor would Italian terrorists kidnapping Italian officials in Italy.

Many of the incidents reported are symbolic bombings not intended to produce casualties but only to dramatize a grievance, publicize a protest, or commemorate some date significant in a political struggle. By type of incident, these bombings show the sharpest increase, which leads to the suspicion that at least part of the overall increase may be due to the existence of a chronology of terrorism and the demand for such information—in short, better reporting. To get around this problem, it is useful to examine incidents with fatalities or injuries (Figure 2), the total number of fatalities (Figure 3), and "major incidents" (Figure 4). Major incidents would include those involving at least one fatality or a number of seriously injured. In the case of a hostage incident, it would involve government officials or demands upon governments. If a hijacking, the hijacker or hijackers would demand something more than simply changing the destination of the aircraft. These criteria would exclude token acts of violence, kidnappings of businessmen, many of the hijackings, and a number of unsuccessful assassinations and kidnappings.

In each case, although the location of the peaks and valleys may differ, the overall trend is still upward, except for major incidents which appear to level off in the mid-1970s. All of these totals are combined in Figure 5 which theoretically should give us at least an impression of the rise of international terrorism of the last decade.

Figure 1. Total number of incidents of international terrorism by year based upon author's chronology

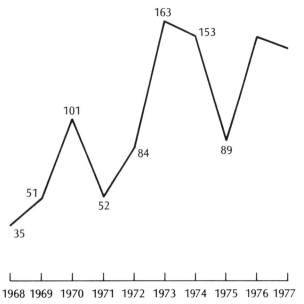

Figure 2. Total number of incidents of international terrorism involving fatalities or injuries by year

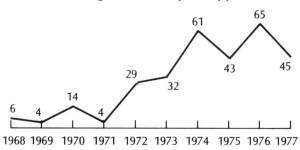

Figure 3. Total number of fatalities in incidents of international terrorism by year

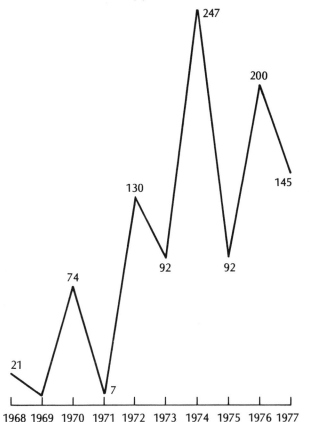

Figure 4. Number of "major incidents" of international terrorism by year

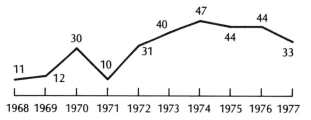

Figure 5. Total number of incidents, incidents with casualties, "major incidents" of international terrorism, and number of casualties, by year

It is noteworthy that this representation does not exactly accord with the public's perceptions of the problem of terrorism nor with government reaction. To illustrate the point, the total number of incidents of international terrorism in 1972 was less than that of 1970, while the number of major incidents was about the same for the two years. Incidents with casualties and the number of deaths caused by terrorists were up in 1972. However, it was two particularly shocking incidents in 1972, the Lod Airport massacre in May and the Munich incident in September, that appalled the world and provoked many governments including the United States to undertake more serious measures to combat terrorism.

Similarly, the year 1975 was labeled by many in the news media as the "year of the terrorist." Certainly 1975 seemed to surpass previous years in the number of dramatic and shocking episodes that occurred. There were continued kidnappings in Latin America and in the Middle East, while in Europe two attempts to shoot down airliners at

Orly Field in Paris, the kidnapping of a candidate for mayor in West Berlin, the seizure of embassies in Stockholm, Kuala Lumpur, and Madrid, the Irish Republican Army's bombing campaign in London, the assassination of the Turkish ambassadors in Austria and France, the hijacking of a train in The Netherlands, the takeover of the Indonesian consulate in Amsterdam, and the seizure of the OPEC oil ministers in Vienna all combined to produce an enormous effect. Certainly, it seemed international terrorism had increased. However, measured by the number of incidents, the number of major incidents, the total number of incidents with casualties, and the total number of casualties, it had in fact declined.

Some observers found encouragement in a seeming "downward trend" in 1976. In fact, however, more incidents of terrorism took place in 1976 and that year was bloodier than 1975. There were more bombings and assassinations, and hijackings, after declining, went up again.

Some continued to perceive a decline in the early months of 1977 but by the end of the year, judging by the number of news articles, television specials, and concern in government, virtually everyone agreed terrorism was on the rise. In fact, it was not. The figures for 1977 indeed show a slight decline.

How do we explain that terrorism often appears to be increasing when it is declining—appears down when it is up? Perhaps we count the wrong things. More likely, the things we can count do not reflect our perceptions of the phenomenon. Terrorism is not simply what terrorists do, but the effect—the publicity, the alarm—they create by their actions.

Public perceptions of the level of terrorism in the world appear to be determined then not by the level of violence but rather by the quality of the incidents, the location, and the degree of media coverage. Hostage incidents seem to have greater impact than murder, barricade situations more than kidnappings. Hostage situations may last for days, possibly weeks. Human life hangs in the balance. The whole world watches, and waits. By contrast, a death, even many deaths, are news for only a few days. They lack suspense and are soon forgotten. More people recall the hijacking of a TWA airliner by Croatian extremists in September 1976 than recall the bomb placed aboard a Cubana airliner three weeks later. No one died aboard the TWA airliner (although a policeman was killed attempting to defuse a bomb planted on the ground by the hijackers). Seventy-three persons died in the crash of the Cubana plane.

The location of the incident is also important. Incidents that occur in cities have more impact than those that occur in the countryside. Incidents in Western Europe and North America seem more important, at least to the American public, than incidents in Latin America, Africa, or Asia. It is a matter of communications. An unseen and unheard terrorist incident produces no effect. The network of modern electronic communications laces Western Europe and North America more thoroughly than the rest of the world. We also tend to exhibit a higher tolerance for terrorist violence in the Third World. Terrorist violence in modern industrial societies with democratic governments jars this bias.

Finally, timing is important. Terrorist violence is easily submerged by higher levels of conflict. Individual acts of violence lose their meaning in a war. It is hard to say how many individual acts of terrorism there were during the war in Indochina or how many individual murders, how many kidnappings there were during the civil war in Lebanon. Even a war in another part of the globe can drown out an act of terrorism. There is only so much time and space for news. Terrorist acts in succession produce the effect of a wave of terrorism but must not crowd each other too closely for world attention lest their impact be diluted.

The past record of terrorism provides no basis for forecasting the future course of terrorism. The fact that international terrorism has increased fitfully during the last decade does not mean that it will continue to increase, or that it will not decline, however we assess the phenomenon. One can say simply that terrorism is likely to persist.

Will terrorists escalate their violence? By this, we mean not the volume of terrorist activity but the things that terrorists do. Measured against the world volume of "ordinary" violence, the amount of terrorist violence up to now has been trivial. Nevertheless, terrorists have been able to attract worldwide attention to themselves and to their causes and produce alarm, and they have achieved these results with tactics that, although shocking, have not killed hundreds or thousands. In the ten years between 1968 and 1977, there were 1,019 incidents of international terrorism in which 1,017 persons were killed and 2,509 persons were wounded or injured, including terrorists. About one person per incident was the average. Actually, only 303 incidents involved any casualties. Putting aside the plane crashes and assaults like that at the Lod and Rome airports, it is apparent that terrorists for the most part have so far avoided indiscriminate attacks that cause widespread casualties. Although many terrorist attacks may have been indiscriminate, they were limited, and in only a few instances did they cause heavy casualties.

Terrorists bent upon mass murder can choose from a variety of means. ("Mass murder" is not a precise term. It is arbitrarily defined here as something approaching 100 or more potential deaths. Conceivably thousands could be imperiled by some of the actions described, but those actions would be extremely difficult to carry out successfully.) Chemical and biological weapons are generally seen as the easiest and most available way to kill a large number of people. A crude nuclear explosive device, depending on its yield and where and when it was detonated, could cause casualties of greater magnitude, but the acquisition of the requisite material and the fabrication of the device would require greater risks and technical skill than either chemical or biological weapons. The dispersal of radioactive material would involve fewer difficulties in the acquisition of the materials, and the fabrication of a dispersal device is far easier than an explosive device, but the probable effects are likely to be exceeded by an effective dispersal of chemical toxins or biological agents.

In the case of both chemical and biological weapons, apart from some difficulties involved with large-scale dissemination, the primary constraints are not technical ones. Toxins can be obtained or manufactured; biological pathogens can be purchased or stolen and cultivated; home laboratories suffice; technical literature is widely available; and many persons possess the necessary skills.

Moral considerations and political utility provide the most important constraints. The fact that most nations have renounced chemical and biological warfare may suggest to any group considering their use that their action will provoke widespread revulsion and foreclose sanctuary. Of course, it can be argued that most terrorist acts provoke widespread revulsion anyway; therefore this cannot be considered a constraint.

The political utility of widespread casualties is not fully demonstrated or necessarily apparent. As a threat, chemical and biological weapons believed to be in the hands of terrorists would have considerable value. The actual use of such weapons, however, might be politically counterproductive. Except as an act of revenge or of extreme desperation where moral constraints and arguments based on political utility erode, it is hard to see why terrorists would believe that mass casualties would serve their cause. One can more easily imagine their use against a more limited target composed of some segment of the population or representative of the system despised by the terrorists—a church, a police station, a government office, the boardroom of a major corporation.

The primary utility of a nuclear weapon would be as an instrument of coercion. With it, terrorists could create a mass hostage situation of unprecedented proportions. But, it is not clear what enormous demand might be made that would be commensurate with a threat of this scale. Springing a handful of prisoners or collecting a few million dollars in ransom does not warrant the investment and risks necessary to fabricate a nuclear weapon. At the other end of the spectrum, certain demands are impossible to satisfy, no matter what the threat. A government, for example, would not agree to liquidate itself. Demands made by terrorists with a nuclear weapon would also have to be of a finite nature, that is, the authors of the threat would have to demand an action or a decision that could not be reversed once the threat had been removed and that could be carried out fairly quickly.

This does not overlook the fact that there are in the world lunatics and crazy political fanatics who might find blowing up a city, or threatening to blow up a city, an attractive undertaking. Their reasons for doing so might, by any other view of the world than their own, be totally bizarre. Fortunately, the requirements for fabricating a nuclear weapon are likely to exceed their capabilities, at least for now and the immediate future. We have not yet reached the time when any bright lunatic can make an atomic bomb, but as plutonium and highly enriched uranium become more widely available and the opportunities for theft or diversion increase, and as the knowledge of how to use them in nuclear weapons becomes more widespread, it is conceivable that a small group, unconcerned for a large constituency, unhindered by the requirements of political logic, pursuing some mad goal, might be able to acquire a nuclear capability and be willing to use it.

When it comes to slaughter, however, terrorists actually have little need for exotic or sophisticated weapons. They have already demonstrated their knowledge of explosives. Bombings are the principal form of terrorist activity. Detonated at places of assembly—railroad and subway stations, bus terminals, aircraft—conventional explosives can cause heavy casualties. But for all their bombings, terrorists thus far have seldom used explosives in ways calculated to kill great numbers of any civilian population. Nor have terrorists ordinarily used the primitive but potentially even more lethal weapon of fire against people. Finally, some of the individual weapons now being developed for tomorrow's infantrymen—man-portable surface-to-air missiles, for example—seem potentially useful to terrorists and, used against certain categories of targets, are capable of causing heavy casualties.

Several incidents have already occurred which suggest this is a real possibility. In 1973, Italian police arrested five Arab terrorists who were planning to shoot down an El Al airliner at the Rome airport. The terrorists had two Soviet-made heat-seeking ground-to-air missiles. Another attempt involving ground-to-air missiles was foiled at the Nairobi airport in 1976. In the fall of 1977, West German terrorists threatened to shoot down or plant bombs aboard Lufthansa airliners in retaliation for the deaths of three of their comrades who had committed suicide in prison. Bombs planted by terrorists were responsible for several airliner crashes in the past decade. In one case, 88 persons died, in another, 73.

Thus, while the potential for mass violence involving the use of a nuclear device or chemical or biological weapons understandably causes the most concern, there is an intermediate level of violence where a few attacks could cause tremendous alarm. Bombs aboard aircraft, sabotage of trains, bombs in terminals and lobbies, and the like could cause up to several hundred casualties. Such attacks pose no technical problems to terrorists, who have on a few occasions mounted attacks of this type. Several such incidents producing several hundred deaths each, although still trivial when compared with the world volume of violence, would bring terrorism into an entirely new dimension.

What other trends can we foresee? One possible development is the emergence of a semi-permanent subculture of terrorism. As succeeding generations of terrorists replace those arrested or killed and acquire a following of active supporters, groupies, sympathizers, lawyers, propagandists, and chroniclers—all in some way dependent on the survival of the terrorist group and the continuation of its activities—it may become a political underworld that is able to survive the fate of any specific terrorist group. It may develop its own service industries providing illegal documents and weapons, as well as fences for stolen cash or ransoms. Terrorism itself may become its ideology.

On the international level we already see that terrorists with quite different goals are able to cooperate with each other, not solely because of ideological affinity, but increasingly so, it seems, on a purely professional basis. They help each other because they are all terrorists.

Today's terrorist groups may become tomorrow's new Mafias, as political objectives become secondary to maintaining a cash flow. The Irish Republican Army, for example, is heavily into extortion; it runs protection rackets, participates in defrauding insurance companies, and also is acquiring ownership of legitimate businesses.

New sources of terrorist violence may emerge. Technological advance appears to be stimulating a powerful resistance which has in some cases turned violent. The increased centralization of the modern state, a reflection of technological advance, has provoked cultural backlash in many countries—an increasing awareness of, and desire to preserve, ethnic identity and autonomy. The last few years have seen the emergence of "neo-Luddites" or, as one European author calls them, "neo-Rousseaunians" who directly challenge modern industrial society's conception of progress. Political extremists in Western Europe have attacked computers and nuclear reactors as the symbols and sinews of modern society. In some cases, the threats of separatism and environmentalism have come together, as in France and Spain, where Breton and Basque separatists have bombed nuclear reactors in support of ethnic autonomy and environmentalist movements.

One immediate effect of the growing threat posed by terrorism, along with other forms of politically motivated violence during the past decade, has been a major diversion of resources to internal security functions. The protection of political leaders and diplomats, airports, portions of the energy system, and other vital systems will continue to demand increasing manpower and money. We can foresee the continuing growth of what we might call "internal defense" budgets as well as of security expenditures by private business. This is part of a major shift in society from viewing security in terms of secure national frontiers, clearly a national responsibility, to the defense of "inner perimeters"—guarded facilities, privately patrolled communities, security buildings, alarmed homes—where the burden of defense is increasingly placed upon local government, the private sector, and the individual citizen.

A second effect of terrorism has been a growing corpus of law to deal with politically motivated crime, specifically acts of terrorism. In many cases, terrorism has been identified as a crime different from, and in most cases more serious than, the traditional crimes that terrorists commit—murder, kidnapping, arson. New criminal offenses, such as air piracy, have been identified. Many countries have extended their penal codes to cover crimes committed outside of the national territory, such as crimes aboard airliners. Legislation has also broadened police powers. In some countries, trial procedures have been changed, generally to the accused's disadvantage. Several nations have created groups at the national level to coordinate national efforts against terrorists. New special anti-terrorist organizations have been created within police departments or within internal security organizations. Military participation in police functions has increased. Private security services have grown tremendously. Special military units for possible use in anti-terrorist operations abroad have also been created in a number of countries.

Although the measures enacted to combat terrorism have impeded free movement to a certain degree, subjected travelers to more scrutiny, and on occasion created a nuisance, we cannot say that democracy has been imperiled by them. Authoritarian regimes have characteristically reacted with repressive measures. Nations with strong democratic traditions have cautiously limited certain liberties as the price of security. As long as terrorism persists, there will continue to be clashes between the perceived need for increased social controls and the protection of individual liberties.

ABOUT THE AUTHORS

Stephen Sloan is Professor of Political Science at the University of Oklahoma. Dr. Sloan has engaged in research in Indonesia and Israel and was a Fulbright Lecturer in Nepal. He has written extensively on international terrorism and has conducted a number of simulations of terrorist incidents at domestic and foreign sites with military and police forces. One of his exercises has been incorporated into the training program of a major airline.

Richard Shultz is Assistant Professor of Political Science at Northern Illinois University, where he teaches International Relations and Foreign and Defense Policy. His major research interests include political terrorism, insurgency and counterinsurgency warfare. Dr. Shultz has written articles and reviews for *Polity, Journal of Peace Research, International Behavioral Scientist, The Annals* and *Western Political Quarterly*. He is currently working on a book concerned with United States counterinsurgency strategies implemented during the Vietnam War. He received his Ph.D. from Miami University.

Major Bard E. O'Neill, United States Air Force, has a Ph.D. in International Relations from the Graduate School of International Studies, Denver University. He is currently the Director of Middle Eastern Studies at The National War College. Major O'Neill is the author of *Revolutionary Warfare in the Middle East* (1974), co-editor and contributor to *Political Violence and Insurgency: A Comparative Approach* (1975), and co-editor of and contributor to *The Energy Crisis and U.S. Foreign Policy* (1975). He has just completed his fourth book, *Armed Struggle in Palestine*.

Richard Ned Lebow has taught Political Science at The City College of the City University of New York and strategy at the Naval War College. He is author of *Divided Nations in a Divided World* (1974), *White Britain and Black Ireland: The Influence of Stereotypes on Colonial Policy* (1976) and *Between Peace and War: The Anatomy of International Crisis* (forthcoming).

Robert K. Mullen received his Ph.D. from the University of Southern California. He is an independent consultant to various Federal, state and private agencies, and industry in matters concerning safeguards appropriate to technologies in advanced, developing and underdeveloped international arenas; national and subnational proliferation potentials inherent in civil nuclear fuel cycles; concepts involving application of mass destruction capabilities among nonaligned powers; and, activities of a similar genre. He resides in Washington, D.C. and Santa Barbara, California.

Paul A. Tharp, Jr., is Associate Professor of Political Science at the University of Oklahoma. Dr. Tharp holds both the J.D. and Ph.D. degrees. In the Political Science Department he teaches courses on international law and organization, and national security.

Yonah Alexander teaches at the University of New York in Oneonta where he is also director of the Institute for Studies in International Terrorism. The editor of *International Terrorism: National, Regional and Global Perspectives* (1976) and author of numerous articles on this topic, Dr. Alexander is also Editor-in-Chief of *Terrorism: An International Journal*.

Brian M. Jenkins is the author of numerous articles and monographs on international terrorism, and is currently a research associate at the Rand Corporation.

INDEX

DATE DUE

		APR 1 4 1989	
~~NOV 27~~		FEB 1 7 2002	
~~DEC 1 1~~ 1980		APR 2 2 2003	
~~MAY 2 0 1981~~			
~~JUN 1 1 1981~~			
~~APR 1 1982~~			
MAY 2 0 1982			
APR 7 1983			
APR 7 1983			
NOV 1 4 1985			
DEC 1 2 1985			
MAR 3 1988			
APR 1 4 1989			

HIGHSMITH 45-220